REVIVING A DYING CHURCH

James McAlister

Copyright 2015
by
James W. McAllister

ISBN 978-1-940609-23-2 Softcover

All rights reserved. No part of this book may be reproduced or transmitted in any form or by any means, electronic or mechanical, including photocopying, recording, or by any information storage and retrieval system, without permission in writing from the copyright owner. All scripture verses are from the King James and New King James Versions of the Bible.

This book was printed in the United States of America.

FWB Publications
Columbus, Ohio

FWB

Table of Contents

About The Author 5
Dedication 7
Forward 9
Preface 13
Part One 15
   The Dying Church 17
Part Two 35
   The Pastor's Role, In Reviving The Church 37
   The Role Of The Lay Leader 51
Part Three 59
   Strategies: Planting The Seeds Of Revival 61
   Strategies: Programming For Revival 71
   Strategies: Preparing Leaders 89
   Strategies: Building God's Church 99
   Strategies: Opening The Altars Of The Church 121
Part Four 139
   Continuity: Understanding The Cycles Of Growth .. 141
   Continuity: Making The Church The Center Of Influence .. 149
   Continuity: Testing The Leadership 161
   Continuity: Keeping The Church Balanced For The Future 173
   Continuity: Obeying The Whole Commission Of Christ 185
A Final Word 195

About the Author

I was born in one of earth's most beautiful places. You haven't seen anything until you have seen an Ozark dogwood in April or the woods in October when the colors are bright and the air is crisp. Missouri! What a beautiful and wonderful state.

I was born again in a small country church outside Lebanon, Missouri. Its name explained what happened when I found Jesus: Liberty. My grandparents were common people of the country, and my parents were a couple that spent their time expressing their love for "Jimmy Bill." That's me!

One day I met the girl of my dreams and I wandered no more. In 1956, Helen and I were married. She is truly the light of my life and my best friend. Everybody knows she is "the German," and as straight as an arrow. God blessed us with four children: Greg, Tambra, Jennifer, and Stacia. (It is Greg who has taken the ramblings of an old man and put them together in this book.) They married Debbie, Roger, Reed, and Tim. Our grandchildren are my beloved ones: Mark, Eric, Rachel, Cody, Caleb, Gabriel, Sunny, Leah (she only stayed with us three months), Caitlin, and Hannah. And I can't forget my brother, Jack. What a beautiful and great family. Thank you Lord!

God has also blessed me with the opportunities to plan and help plant seven churches. In every church I started, and in the five churches I've pastored for the past forty-six years, I've had wonderful people surrounding and loving me. I thank God for each of these precious people.

My family, my congregations and my Lord have taught me all I know about pastoring.

I would like to express special appreciation to my son, Greg. As I wrote earlier, he has done so much to fix this book for publication. He has been with me in my pastorates, my administration at California Christian College, and in my writing. I depend on him so much. Thank you, and God bless you, son!

Dedication

To my wife and family

To the Lord for His call on my life

To the churches and people I have had the privilege to pastor.

James McAlister

Forward

Many pastors are convinced that it is far better to start new churches than to revive the struggling dying church. I admit that it is much easier to give birth than to resurrect the dead, but the fact remains that there are thousands of dying churches that could be revived if the right pastor had the right vision and used the right tools.

The first step is conviction- becoming convinced that there is a problem. Are churches really dying? Is there anything to be concerned about? It is my opinion that death begins where growth ceases. Therefore, a church that is not growing is dying.

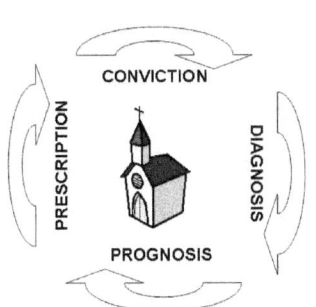

PROCESS FOR REVIVING THE DYING CHURCH

The second step is diagnosis- determining why churches do not grow. I believe we can safely say that pastors and members kill churches. They program themselves for failure in ministry. They set second-rate priorities, base decisions on faulty assumptions, and solve the wrong problems. Weak leadership directs the church away from growth.

The third step is prognosis- deciding what can be done to save the life of the church. In general, the ingredients necessary to revive a congregation include strong leadership, renewed zeal, goals, obedience, cooperation, personal responsibility, and solid organization. I'm sure you could add your own items, based on your own experience.

The fourth step is prescription- determining which programs should be undertaken and in what order. As a result of study and personal experience, I believe these objectives should be pursued (the order in which they are pursued depends on your particular situation):

- Formulate a plan for revival
- Fully inform the people of the plan
- Lead through example
- Develop lay leadership
- Revise every church program to focus on growth, especially anything having to do with the worship services (music and pulpit ministry) and Christian education.
- Challenge the congregation to take risks
- Pay close attention to the evangelistic strategy (including choosing special speakers who address real spiritual and organizational needs, beginning an evangelistic outreach, and upgrading the bus ministry, if one exists)
- Initiate a one-on-one disciple program for new converts
- Establish sound financial principles.

In short, the ultimate goal is nothing less than a complete reorganization of the entire church- programmatically, spiritually, and effectually. During this long-term process, the "flavor" you give your church will come from continually emphasizing and teaching the principles, methods, and importance of growth. As a result of these efforts, church self-esteem will be restored and spiritual growth will be evident. Numerical growth will follow.

Plenty has already been written on the subject of church growth and revitalization. I see no need to rehash what these writers have already said so well, since, if this subject interests you, you probably already own their books. This work will concentrate only on my own experiences, as well as wisdom I have gathered from close friends and colleagues over the years. Nothing in this book is theory. I have seen it work. I trust you will take what you can use, but I also hope you will grasp the context in which I have ministered for Christ over the past 45 years. You will, however, be able to tell that I was heavily influenced by some very basic principles articulated by Dr. Donald A. McGavran early in my ministry.

This is not a book about how to become a mega-church. It is about turning a congregation around. I have always pastored Free Will Baptist Churches. Every church I have pastored was small at the time I became pastor and grew substantially (New Hope Church- Kansas City, KS [founding pastor], Olivet Church- Marshall, MO [founding pastor], Central Church- Kansas City, MO [founding pastor], First Church- Monett, MO, First Church- Farmington, MO and Harmony Church- Fresno, CA) as a result of the action steps outlined in this work. I believe the steps in this book will be helpful to any pastor who desires to revive a dying church.

Bold, spiritual, well-conceived change is necessary for any church to be revived. Just as disciples need to be able to tell that they are growing in Christ, the congregation needs to be able to see that positive steps are being taken to preserve the work in which they have invested themselves. Bold, spiritual, well-conceived change requires bold, spiritual, well-planned leadership. This is your context. This is your responsibility. This is pastoring.

Preface

Churches in America are dying leaving pastors frustrated because they do not know how to build a church.

Over my 60 years of ministry, I have only known a few pastors who have built a great church. One such person is the author of this book.

Over the course of his years of ministry he has built four large churches from small congregations.

He re-organized these churches to grow, using Biblical principles, teaching the membership in the areas of outreach by reaching into the community, and then using the various components within the church by building the converts and revitalizing members that had sat desolate for so long.

This book describes the problem with most local churches, but the author does not leave one hanging as he defines and designs the programs that assisted in rebuilding these churches.

I am privileged to recommend this book which will aid you and help you raise from any stagnation in your church.

Dr. Alton E. Loveless

PART ONE

Definitions

Not every pastor would recognize a dying church if they looked at one. When we get used to things, they become invisible. This section provides a definition of the dying process churches go though.

DEFINITION: THE DYING CHURCH

And now for a little space grace hath been showed from the LORD our God, to leave us a remnant to escape, and to give us a nail in his holy place, that our God may lighten our eyes, and give us a little reviving in our bondage.--Ezra 9:8

There is a dearth of thriving, soul winning churches across the United States. Conservative, Biblicist believers often spend time arguing about whether we are evangelicals or fundamentalists. We discuss the varieties and divisions of both groups. We spend a great deal of time debating the merits of different positions on the deeper life, eschatology, and degrees of separation. The world is on fire, burning with lust and deceit. Evil men are taking over. Wickedness abounds everywhere. While the house burns, we are painting the porch. While souls are tormented by the devil, we give back-rubs. A pastor I know has a picture of a small church with weeds growing all around the doors, and with the windows and doors boarded up. In the yard was a large sign reading, "Closed due to sin." In an old eastern Kansas town, a mainline denomination church closed and the property was taken over by a tavern. The tavern was named, appropriately, "Ichabod," which means, "The glory is departed."

If it is true that the Lord gave the church for the purpose of reaching the unreached, if he established the church to edify those who have been saved, then the church should be about the Father's business. Is the church conscientiously carrying out that purpose? In a 1976 conference in Kansas City, MO, Dr. Donald McGavran argued that four of every five churches in America were in the process of dying. For years Robert Shockey, a close friend and evangelist, illustrated the urgency of his mission by saying that every time a meal was eaten, three times a day, another church closed its doors and went out of business.

Symptoms of Churches in Critical Condition

Dying churches can be identified by at least seven very noticeable signs.

1. The altars are bare. Not only are sinners seldom seen mourning over their sins and repenting, but Christians also shy away from the altar. Weeks will go by without anyone coming forward. One pastor joked that he preached thirteen weeks in a row and the only people who came forward were the ushers.
2. There is little evangelistic outreach, either in neighborhoods, on a one-on-one basis, or through foreign missions. Some churches attempt to salve their consciences by giving to missions, thereby excusing their lack of community outreach, but that is a shallow effort. People who do not care about the souls of those in the community will not continue caring about those in other nations.
3. There is growing financial plight. Budgets soon decrease as inflation rises, members move away, become inactive, change churches or die, and new members are not brought in to take up the slack. Programs and salaries are inevitably cut back, which discourages volunteers and staff members.

4. Attendance will dwindle. Low attendance hinders all phases of the ministry- finances, music, outreach, mission giving, and morale. Small attendance is discouraging to those who do come, influencing them to look elsewhere. Low attendance burdens a few people with multiple responsibilities, or allows some members to exercise control. Small numbers also force ministers to find reasons for small numbers to salvage self-esteem, which usually ends up in a narrow view of God's will or spiritual gifts.
5. The facilities show signs of decay. Before long members simply do not care about the church property, or don't even notice its state of disarray. Prospective members relate the lack of property care to a probable lack of pastoral care, and don't even consider visiting, much less becoming members.
6. Spiritual carelessness and worldliness will grow as attendance decreases. A coroner's rule of thumb is "Corruption is absolute proof of death" (Emma Lathen). One of the fallback positions for pastors of small churches is the myth that small churches are somehow holier than large churches, similar to the cliché that small towns are somehow more wholesome than large cities. Just as small towns can conceal grisly crimes, some very ungodly people may attend the small churches where no one cares. Since the small church can barely afford to pay the pastor's salary, it certainly cannot afford to risk offending any tithers, no matter what their behavior may be.
7. There will be disunity. When all else fails, so does harmony. People who are genuinely concerned about their church's decline but do not know what to do

about it, or are waiting in vain for their leadership to lead, will begin looking for reasons, and after a while may simply start assigning blame.

A dying church may not have all these signs of death, but it will definitely exhibit some of them. A dead church will probably have all of them. Churches are dying from California to North Carolina, from Alaska to Florida, and the results are devastating. Millions of lost souls, shame and reproach on the name of Christ and His church, family breakups, and juvenile delinquency are just a few of the terrible consequences of church death.

It is necessary to decide how to define the term "dying church." Church growth-oriented pastors will agree that any church that stops growing soon begins to die. As this concept is considered closely, it becomes obvious that there are different degrees of "dying." When a church is labeled as "dying," that doesn't mean it is dead. It may mean that the congregation has lost, or is losing, its concern for the lost people of the community. It may mean that division and strife has set in and there is no longer a spirit of unity. It may be years before it gasps its last breath, but it is dying. The finer points of this question may be argued, but it is important to realize that the spiritual cemeteries of the world are strewn with the skeletons and drying bones of dying and dead churches.

It is also important to remember that any time an institution ceases to grow, it begins to die. Someone once said, "Growth for the sake of growth is the theology of the cancer cell." For many pastors, this justifies non-growth. Pastors convinced of the imperative of the Great Commission do not believe in growth for the sake of growth. Growth represents souls reached for Christ. Converts have to be preserved somewhere. The only method God gave us for discipling converts is the church. It is hypocritical to downplay the importance of church growth at the same time we teach that souls must be saved. Senator Paul Tsongas once said to the Democratic Party, "You can't be pro-job and anti-business." In like manner, we can't be pro-Christ and anti-Church growth. It just doesn't work. If we don't emphasize growth, growth won't happen. Any time anything stops growing, it starts dying. That's just the way it is.

Pastoral Mistakes

People kill churches. Leaders halt growth and thus provoke the death of the local church. Churches die because of blind leadership. There is no vision. The leader who does not promote an individual and collective prayer life, Bible study, worship, and evangelism will soon see the signs of church death.

Pastors can make major mistakes that are hardly noticeable at the time, but the long-term consequences are very noticeable. As a pastor for over forty-five years, I can now see how I injured churches, and sometimes hindered their growth by doing little things that didn't seem to matter much at the time, but had long-term effects. Little foxes do indeed spoil the vines (Song of Solomon 2:15).

There are some symptoms pastors develop when they are making major mistakes.

For one thing, we become obsessed with problems. Problems literally become all we talk about. Because of this obsession, we begin to rationalize our decisions, trying to vindicate ourselves and assign blame to others. We tend to believe in a "silver bullet," a single method, decision, or policy that will solve all the problems in our church, which leads to impulsive decisions. These misconceptions can be corrected, but only by being realistic. We have to find the real cause of the problem. Unfortunately, we usually settle for identifying the cause of our problems as a person, and his or her actions, attitude, and participation or lack thereof. This person is singled out as the great enemy, and we begin zeroing in on his or her conspiracy against us and, therefore, God and His Church. We become hypersensitive to every facial expression, comment, act, missed service, vote, and mistake of this supposed enemy. Growth is no longer the desire of our heart. Solving the problem is our only goal, and usually the solution we conceive involves getting rid of the problem person. It is possible that this analysis is true, but it can also be a symptom of denial. Isaiah admitted that he was the one in need of prayer, and that is the first step toward curing an obsession. The pastor who is patient, loving, and determined about the goals chosen for the church can outlast just about any opposition.

I have found that opposition eventually gets tired if I am convinced that my goals have integrity and am willing to be loving all the while. I believe that, under those circumstances, problem people usually leave the church when it will benefit the church the most. In fact, the pastor who focuses on vision instead of problems rarely loses anyone the church doesn't need to lose. I also believe that problem people serve an important purpose in a church. For one thing, they provide an example of what a loyal church member isn't. They also hold the pastor to a standard. I am less likely to say frivolous things in a sermon, take radical positions on a whim, or be ill-prepared for a meeting when I know my critic is licking his lips, hoping I stumble.

Pastors minimize their own leadership role. It should not be surprising that a church suffers when a strong pastor-leader resigns. Leaders, whether strong or weak, determine the course of the church. Churches rise or fall on pastoral leadership. A strong pastor-leader brings growth and inspiration to a new church, and unless another strong leader follows him, a dying congregation will result from his departure. Wherever he goes, growth and enthusiasm follow.

The servant-leadership concept, while Christ-like, has been critically misinterpreted and misapplied over the years. It is common to find a pastor who refuses to make any decisions for fear of imposing his will on a church, which is "anti-servant hood." It almost seems as though they believe that indecisiveness is godly. This interpretation is illogical. If God has appointed someone as leader of a church, and that is what a pastor is, to not lead is ridiculous. It ignores the fact that leadership and administration are gifts of the Holy Spirit. And believe me, if a pastor refuses to lead, someone else will. Someone always steps up to the plate, because human beings demand leadership; i.e., they demand to be led. Jesus wept over Israel because they were "sheep without a shepherd." It may even be sinful to forego leadership responsibilities if you have been appointed pastor.

Fear of failure creates control issues. We may fear failure so much that we hold on to the church so tightly we squeeze the life right out of it. We do not allow laymen to use their gifts of service and leadership. We want to do everything, lead everything, and be praised for everything. And so, we are afraid to take risks. We only make decisions we are sure will not hurt us if we fail. Failure is the greatest teacher there is. I have actually learned very little from my successes, because I tend to forget how they were accomplished- rose-colored glasses, and all that. But I never forget a failure. Failure is the gift that goes on giving. Failure can be resented and feared, or it can be valued as the lesson it is.

Besides, failures point out what won't work, so you don't waste time trying it again in the future. As Thomas Edison is supposed to have said after thousands of tries, "Now I know thousands of ways not to make a light bulb." Fear of failure creates a tendency to keep a tight grip on all decision-making. Granted, no one likes looking silly, but leadership isn't necessarily squandered in a failure. "If you mess up, 'fess up" is a good spiritual principle for a leader, or any believer, to live by. In fact, a pastor who admits his mistakes can actually build leadership capital through a failure. Handling it well can inspire others to attempt great things for God.

Congregational Mistakes
A church may be indifferent to church growth and see growth as an option, instead of a mandate from God. Too many congregations look at their church as a social institution instead of a spiritual hospital. When evangelism is seen as a choice and not a requirement, the worship services are generally geared to meet some other need. The congregation will be active in other areas and the sermons will be directed toward secondary purposes.

A church may produce a church boss who strangles pastoral leadership and refuses to relinquish his or her dictatorial roles. These bosses prefer that the church remain small enough to be controllable, rather than become too large to control. Sixty is about as many people as anyone can control, and the average church has about sixty people in it. I don't know if I can draw a direct correlation between the two, but it's certainly interesting, isn't it. By the way, these church bosses are often the people who stepped up when a pastor refused to lead.

A church may refuse to do the things that are required for growth, such as providing adequate, usable facilities, or reorganize appropriately for the different stages of church life. It is easier to let a few people do everything than to develop lay leadership, so many churches don't develop beyond the ability of the few leaders they have. Churches are more likely to relocate because of property values than for evangelistic purpose.

A church may tolerate sin in its midst because it is a "family matter." This was a problem with the church in Corinth. Sin must be addressed. That doesn't mean that a pastor can be careless about the feelings of others or have a lack of compassion; but sin cannot be tolerated and addressing it firmly is not cruel. Preaching, by its very nature, is judgmental, because you are communicating God's opinion of sin. As long as the pastor can maintain the time-honored principle of "hate the sin, love the sinner," these situations can be handled.

A church may hold the pastor totally responsible for growth, taking a sort of "hired hand" approach. They blame him for non-growth if nothing happens, and at the same time be doing all they can to thwart his efforts to promote growth. Again, a church rarely loses anyone it doesn't need to lose. A pastor who is willing to take a long while to teach his church and outlive the problems will eventually produce a congregation that holds itself accountable to God for growth.

One major cause for the great number of dying churches is that there are some absolutely essential fundamentals that have been neglected. He mentioned such things as prayer, evangelistic preaching, evangelistic visitation, and training of youth.

After considering much of the resource material available, interviewing several pastors who have watched churches die, and reviewing my own years of pastoral, evangelistic, and denominational ministries, I have reached the conclusion that no one problem alone can kill a church. It takes a combination of problems, both large and small, continually attacking the church through the pastor and the laity, to put a church on the critical list.

Why Churches Die

In order to revitalize a church death, we must first identify reasons for a church death:

Some churches have a vital evangelistic ministry, but have either no follow-up program, or an inadequate follow-up program, for new converts. Converts are spiritual babies, and churches that do not see the responsibility they have for nurture are creating a population of spiritual orphans. Evangelism-discipleship is one essential concept, one process, not a couple of options. I was once told by a neighboring pastor that churches of my denomination can have converts quicker than any other group, but they run out the back door even faster.

The pastor may try to do everything. Pastors like this may be very humble individuals who simply misunderstand the biblical role of the pastor-leader, or they may just crave approval and think being "ubiquitous" will guarantee that the congregation believes they are indispensable. In either case, they prevent themselves from doing what the pastor alone can do (preaching and leading), while occupying positions and doing things the membership must be trained to do. They shorten and limit their own ministries, waste their health, fray their nerves, and waste precious time. They also neglect the training of workers. Both the paid staff and the volunteers are robbed of the precious privilege of doing a great work for God. The church suffers greatly due to this common behavior. I have seen pastors who do everything they pay a staff to do, or insist on telling the staff member every detail of every task, leaving nothing to the staff member's ingenuity. This is a waste of time, talent and salary.

The church does not believe growth is God's will or that non-growth is sin. There is a sociological theory that the reason Americans build our heroes up to the point that they have to fall is a secret assumption that failure is somehow nobler than success, and we want to make sure that everyone operates at the same level- the lowest common denominator. According to this theory, that's why the South loves Elvis so much. He was a poor boy who made good, but he crashed, thereby proving that failure is the norm, and therefore the proper way to live.

It's possible that many American Christians are deeply suspicious of large, successful churches, and therefore actually structure churches to remain small. This may be at the heart of the community emphasis taught in pastoral courses in many evangelical colleges and seminaries. I believe that's nonsense. If we believe that, the culture is influencing us when we should be influencing the culture.

Dr. Donald McGavran spoke at a conference I attended nearly 40 years ago, and the simple explanation he offered for non-growth still resonates with me. I have seen these principles of non-growth proven over and over. Briefly, if a church doesn't grow, at least one of these reasons is the cause:

The church doesn't pray for growth. As an Arminian, with a strong view of the free will of man in relation to God's sovereign plan of salvation, I believe that Christ's Great Commission (Matthew 28:18-20) put an "onus on us"- that is, we have a command to fulfill if the world is to hear of and receive Christ. Anything that important requires much prayer for power, for equipping, for vision and for wisdom. If we don't pray about something, it might imply that we don't take it very seriously that or that we don't think it's our problem. Without question, God is the Only One Who saves; and we are his ministers, with greater works before us, if John 14:12 is true: "Verily, verily, I say unto you, He that believeth on me, the works that I do shall he do also; and greater works than these shall he do; because I go unto my Father."

The church doesn't know what produces church growth. I supposed that the blame for a church that doesn't know what produces growth would lie with the pastor, since he is the leader. He either isn't teaching it, or he doesn't know himself. I remember once inviting a fellow pastor to attend a church growth seminar with me, and he replied, "Jim, I'm not pastoring as well as I know how now." I couldn't really tell if he was joking or not. I have found, over the years, that if people who love God and have a vision for their church find out what produces growth, they jump at the chance to do it. Obviously, not 100% of a congregation is going to go for the vision. As I recall, 8.5% of Christ's disciples didn't buy into the vision either, and only 8.5% followed him to the cross. The Biblical principle is that there is always a remnant, and those are the people the pastor is to locate and lead (Matthew 10:11-13).

The church is not doing the things that produce growth. These are the practical measures I mentioned earlier. The church's primary responsibility here, I suppose, is to keep from doing anything stupid. Wisdom is required to know what to do. The nice thing about wisdom is that anyone who asks for it in faith gets it (James 1:5-8). It is important to note that not everything works everywhere. This is where culture must be considered. Senator Barry Goldwater (Republican, AZ) once admitted in a television interview that he was unelectable in certain parts of the country. His perspective was that what was considered "conservative" in New York would be considered "liberal" in Arizona, and what was conservative in Arizona was considered insane in New York. And what New York considered liberal, was considered communism in Arizona. That's an important perspective to keep in mind, whether you agree with it or not. It is also important to remember that we are not to evangelize people who already agree with Christ, but those who don't. We have to keep their perspective in mind when we choose what to do as growth strategy.

The church doesn't want growth. Sadly, this may be true more often than we like. Church can often be a "comfort zone" for us, and anything new disturbs the comfort. Consider how much havoc a new baby wreaks on a household. There are diapers everywhere, toys everywhere, dirty clothes everywhere, no sleep left undisturbed, no schedule left unchanged- and all this is caused by someone who cannot walk, talk, or feed themselves. A baby disturbs even a household that is prepared for it; consider how it changes a home in which no preparation has been made. Consider how a baby Christian would disturb a church that hasn't had a convert in years, is set in its ways.

I'm a grandfather several times over, and the distance between the two youngest is 8 years. We thought we were through with all that. We no longer had a baby-proof home. Suddenly, here came Hannah, like a crazed demolition derby contestant, blowing through our peaceful home- and we're all too old to keep up with her. It takes all three of my daughters and my son and their families to manage Hannah during holiday gatherings. It's a lot easier to let the young ones worry about the kids. On the other hand, she has added so much joy to our lives- we can't imagine being without her. Our comfort zone is gone, and in its place is a growing, thriving little girl who gets taught and loved and disciplined by the whole family. What a thrill! It's great to feel young again! That's what a church has to look forward to when it renews its mission to evangelize and disciple.

There are some additional reasons for a lack of growth that I have observed over the years, but they are less philosophical than McGavran.

1. The church is not united. There is not a united front opposing the devil and the world. There is no united effort to evangelize the community. There is no unity in love, goals or efforts. There are old hurts, resentments, and irreconcilable differences. It is important to remember that this is a constant within even the growing church. It is common to find people in church who just plain don't like each other, and that pastor will have to constantly monitor who isn't getting along with whom. Any reason is sufficient to not be united.

2. The church has no vision. Proverbs warns, "Where there is no vision the people perish." When a church does not have a vision for souls or growth, it dies. Little is offered to a diverse population beyond Sunday morning services and a softball league. Church doors locked more days during the week than they are unlocked. Services are abbreviated so they are less

intrusive, and focus on entertainment so no one will lose interest during the short time they are there. Churches have little or no community impact; in fact, few beyond the membership may even know the church exists. Many congregations exist for years without ever seeing a soul saved. It would be bad enough if these symptoms were seen once in each town, but that is not the case. Unfortunately, this visionless ecclesiology is the norm. In many cities there is not a single growing, evangelistic, church. No one seems to care, not even the pastor.

3. Pastors are shallow and materialistic. A few years ago a fellow-pastor told me, "If you want to visit my people, go ahead." I couldn't understand his unconcern for his own congregation at the time, but now I'm afraid I do. The average pastor seems to be little different from the average guy working 40 hours per week. He tends to crave security, respectability and a good salary that enables him to live on the same level as the people he golfs or hunts or fishes with. His wife and children want to dress like everyone else. His sons play on the local school basketball team. His daughter is a cheerleader. He belongs to a few local clubs, and is generally accepted as an all-around nice guy. He is active in his area denominational program- he may even hold an office. This, along with his membership in the local ministerial alliance, keeps him busy. He takes vacations, hunts, plays golf, drives a nice car, and dresses to make his congregation proud of him. There is nothing wrong with any of these things, but when they numb our burden for souls and kill our ambition to build God's church, they are wrong. And besides,

blending in isn't exactly the Biblical model for leadership.
4. The laity is unconcerned and materialistic too. The average layman comes to church when it is convenient. He is not nearly as concerned about the church or his attendance there, as he is about his membership in the labor union or his civic club. He will skip services to coach a little league baseball team, or miss a service to entertain a relative. He considers it a chore to serve on a church board, and thinks nothing of missing a meeting. He rebels at high Christian standards and resists indebtedness for the church. He may go on visitation if nagged about it, and tithes out of obligation. He has little loyalty to either the church or the pastor. His wife wants to be a socialite, and his children are like everyone else's children. Because of this unconcern, most churches maintain small attendance, inadequate facilities, low incomes, and little real impact on their communities. It is little wonder that churches are dying. No one seems to care.

It is easy to understand why churches are dying. In fact, given the prevalence of these problems, it is difficult to understand how any churches are growing at all.

Rationale for Rescue

There are those who feel that time and money should not be wasted trying to revive a dying church. They argue that it is "easier to give birth than raise the dead." While that may be true, it is still somewhat cynical and utilitarian. Aren't dying churches worth a rescue effort?

Jim McAlister
REVIVING A DYING CHURCH

Consider the assets a dying church has to offer that a new church project does not possess. The building may not be adequate, but at least it is a place to start. The congregation may be small and uncommitted, but at least there is a core group to organize. The church's reputation may be bad, but at least a few people know about the church. The fact that a church exists means that sometime in its history this congregation has won souls and probably still has a few people who are loyal to the church, love it and pray for it. No new church possesses any of these assets.

The fact that a church is dying does not negate its necessity. Its final demise means that spiritual needs will go unmet. It needs resurrection, ministry fulfillment and purpose. During 1976 evangelism conference in Kansas City, MO, Dr. Donald McGavran said, "There are 400,000 churches in America; yet if everyone were to attend church at one given time, we would first have to build 700,000 new churches." That was 1976. There are nearly 100 million more people in the United States now, due to immigration and birth rates. Sheer population statistics alone prove that the dying church is necessary. Every church that fades from the scene means 300,000-plus new churches must be built to reach this country.

Something must be done to revive these thousands of dying churches and get them started winning the lost. The dying church is necessary, but only if it is revived.

PART TWO

Roles

Understanding who we are in God's plan is vital to making sure our churches survive and thrive. God's approach is that everyone has an equal part to play. This section deals with those roles.

Jim McAlister | 36
REVIVING A DYING CHURCH

ROLES: THE PASTOR-LEADER'S ROLE IN REVIVING THE CHURCH

The elders which are among you I exhort, who am also an elder, and a witness of the sufferings of Christ, and also a partaker of the glory that shall be revealed:

Feed the flock of God which is among you, taking the oversight thereof, not by constraint, but willingly; not for filthy lucre, but of a ready mind.

Neither as being lords over God's heritage, but being examples to the flock.

And when the chief Shepherd shall appear, ye shall receive a crown of glory that fadeth not away.--1 Peter 5:1-4

There is little question that God's work requires strong leadership. Psalm 23 teaches that the shepherd provides all that is necessary for the sheep. He leads them out and goes before them. Sheep require a strong shepherd. When leadership is weak, the result is catastrophe. "And they were scattered, because there is no shepherd: and they became meat to all the beasts of the field, when they were scattered" (Ezekiel 34:5). This verse teaches three things: the sheep were scattered; they were scattered because there was no shepherd; and scattered sheep are always in danger.

The Necessity of Pastoral Leadership

Ezekiel 34:6 lays the blame for scattering on the pastors: "My sheep wandered through all the mountains, and upon every high hill: yea, my flock was scattered upon all the face of the earth, and none did search or seek after them." The primary thrust of this verse is an accusation against the shepherds. They did not search for the lost sheep. They did not love the sheep. Shepherds who do not shepherd…what a terrible indictment! This same indictment could probably be brought against the average pastor today. It is not uncommon to encounter congregations that appear to be unloved, unvisited, unprotected, unfed, and generally neglected by their shepherd. The scene in Ezekiel 34 is shameful and prompts the Lord to declare, "Behold, I am against the shepherds; and I will require my flock at their hand, and cause them to cease from feeding the flock; neither shall the shepherds feed themselves anymore; for I will deliver my flock from their mouth, that they may not be meat for them" (verse 10).

The Bible contains over 500 references to sheep. Sheep symbolized the means for livelihood. They provided sustenance (meat and milk), and shelter (wool for clothing and tents). They were also a medium of exchange and an element of sacrificial worship. Because of the very nature of sheep-submissive, defenseless, in constant need of guidance and care-the Bible often draws an analogy between sheep and believers. Both sheep and believers need a strong leader.

Qualities of a Strong Pastor

One of the underlying principles of my pastoral philosophy is that you are either the pastor, or you're not. In order to fulfill the idea of pastor as presented in the person of Christ and the examples of Scripture, certain qualities are necessities.

The strong leader loves the flock. The term "shepherd" is used in Scripture to refer to sheep owners, sons of owners, or hirelings (hired hands). In John 10:1-15, Jesus presents himself as "the good shepherd," and presents one quality of shepherding as superceding all others: the shepherd loves the sheep. As the under shepherd, the pastor must love his sheep. He must have a genuine commitment to them.

This is not always the case. Christ contrasts Himself with the hireling: "I am the good shepherd: the good shepherd giveth his life for the sheep. But he that is a hireling, and not the shepherd, whose own the sheep are not, seeth the wolf coming, and leaveth the sheep, and fleeth, because he is a hireling and careth not for the sheep. I am the good shepherd, and know my sheep, and am known of mine" (11-15). In other words, the pastor is not a mercenary. He does not care for the sheep because of the paycheck or to fulfill his own self-esteem deficits. He cares for the sheep out of love, because he can do no other. Whenever the pastor serves for any reasons other than deep love for God and the flock, he must be classified as a "hireling," a mercenary.

The loving shepherd is conscientious about his duties toward the flock. The pastor is called to lead the sheep to sustenance, protect the flock from danger, and to lead them into rest. He uses a rod (club) to protect and guard the sheep, and a staff to rescue and direct them.

In Mark 6, when Jesus looked at the people following Him, He saw them as people with no leader, no love, and no life. He was moved with compassion and began to teach them; in effect, He began to shepherd them. He spoke to them of the kingdom of God. He healed them. He taught them. And he fed them, both literally and spiritually. As He did these things,

He acted out His love for them by caring for their needs.

The strong leader must feed himself so he will have spiritual provisions to feed the flock. People come to church with hungry hearts, injuries, and heartaches. They come expecting to be taught, strengthened, encouraged, edified, and fed. The leader must feed them, and this responsibility requires much study. The word for "shepherd" in 1 Peter is "overseer," which implies that the shepherd looks after the sheep, to prevent stragglers, but also looks over the sheep. This means he examines them constantly to check for problems, diseases, or infestations. It also suggests that he looks beyond the sheep. That means he sees further than the sheep; because he stands taller than the sheep- they have different horizons. The pastor sees further than the flock because he has a different perspective- even while standing among the sheep. He has to seek what God wants first, as well as where God's provisions are.

The strong pastor sets the right example. God's man sets examples for the flock by his prayer life, Bible study, family life, manner of dress, language, attitude, emotions, finances and general life style. This can be a problem, because many pastors are simply lazy. In one of Jesus' parables the master condemned a servant who hid his talent because he claimed to be afraid and of failure. The master saw through his excuse and condemned him as a "wicked and slothful servant" (Matthew 25:28). In the ministry, laziness is wickedness. The pastor cannot live a leisurely lifestyle, sleeping until 9:00 a.m., spending the morning at home reading the mail and the paper, and then run around town doing errands or amusing himself playing golf. He must be busy- in his office, on the job, among his people. If he is to have credibility, his people must know he is not lazy.

The strong pastor must be unafraid to take his leadership role.

Leadership is a frightening thing. Moses tried to evade his call to lead by claiming he was a poor speaker, that he had no credibility, that the people wouldn't listen because they didn't know who God was, and that the people themselves were unworthy of the effort.

Joshua was afraid of the challenge of filling Moses' shoes. God constantly had to admonish him to "be not afraid." The tenure in the pastorate is always uncertain. This causes fear, which breaks a person down both physically and emotionally. Pastors are harassed, slandered, ridiculed and rejected. They receive a mandate to preach the whole council of God, realizing at the same time that their success is likely to be limited to their popularity. He must shoulder the whole burden and depend completely on the Lord. The stress is unreal. The job description requires him to be disciplinarian, negotiator, visionary, auditor, administrator and public relations director. Yes, there is much to fear.

Paul was afraid of the responsibility. He referred to the burden and responsibility of the pastor as unique among all the pressures he faced (2 Corinthians 11:19-33). But the call to lead must be accepted, and the fear it brings must be conquered. The pastor will make mistakes, but he must move beyond the fear of failure and continue to lead, because the call is divine (Romans 1:14) and direct (Isaiah 55:4). It is an awesome responsibility, this call to lead, but the man of God must accept it willingly, joyfully, knowingly, and bravely.

The shepherd is accountable for every sheep. None can be lost or forgotten. This requires a personal investment of time, attention and concern. There is a call to witness to the people, to lead the people, and to command the people in Isaiah 55:4. In like manner, the congregation has the responsibility to obey the admonitions of the pastor because he has responsibility for the souls of the congregation before God (Hebrews 13:17).

The strong pastor will be a man of vision. He must have learned from his experience (successes and failures), what the current condition of the congregation is, and where the church needs to go. He must visualize a packed church, altars filled with mourners, and busses rolling in loaded with people. He must visualize the baptistery waters troubled every week. In his heart, he must see hundreds joining the church membership. He must visualize new facilities to meet the needs produced by his vision. He must visualize generous missions giving, and men and women responding to God's call to spread the gospel. He must be a visionary.

The strong pastor must be holy. There is no greater requirement than holiness for God's chosen leader. "A baptism of holiness, a demonstration of godly living, is the crying need of our day" (Duncan Campbell). God's man must regularly retreat from daily life, fast, pray and meditate in the Scripture until the heavens are opened and the power of God falls. That cannot happen to one who views holiness lightly. The pastor must see himself as utterly helpless without the divine touch from heaven. That is how he demonstrates to the members of the congregation that they are utterly helpless without that same divine touch.

The strong pastor is content to be a shepherd. Far too many pastors have a hidden desire to be evangelists, a denominational big shots, college professors, rich and famous, or just about anything else but a simple pastor. A strong leader must be content to pastor God's church, and see this as the highest calling. The former president of one of my denomination's colleges told the pastoral candidates, "If God has called you to preach, you will be unwilling to stoop to become the President of the United States. And if you can do anything else besides pastor and be right with God, you should do it."

The strong pastor must be a competent leader. Knowing how to lead is a requirement for any pastor. It is true that there are many natural talents and abilities, but these abilities must be acquired and sharpened if the pastor is to truly be effective. There has never been a time when leadership was in more demand, but there is also no shortage of books and training available on this subject. A simple study of the leaders in the Bible may be the most productive professional undertaking a pastor could have.

When Robert F. Kennedy addressed the monthly meeting of the Protestant Episcopal Diocese of Washington, DC in 1963, he said, "If I have learned anything in the last two years in working on the local level, it is that when the clergy provide leadership, we can move ahead." Attorney General Kennedy was speaking of clergy involvement in the civil rights movement. It is sad that clergy often fail to provide leadership in the arena to which they are called, the church. If the pastor provides adequate leadership, the church moves ahead. No leadership means-no success.

Learning to Lead

One of the great myths of pastoring is that leadership is based on personality or unusual gifts. I have little doubt that there are unusually gifted leaders, but I also believe that there are very few people who cannot lead, each according to the measure God has given them. We look for born leaders, but Christ advocated discipling leaders. This was his preferred way of developing leaders. Perhaps you have no access to a mentor who can disciple you into leadership, but you have many

resources at your disposal:

Learn to lead by reading Christ's leadership material. The gospels are records of the discipling of the apostles. The epistles are the records of the discipling the apostles did. We have access to the greatest spiritual leadership material conceivable- the very mind of Christ and the apostles. By the way, if you are five or fewer years from retirement from the ministry, you will probably be tempted to coast. It is a lot of effort to read and prepare and think about leading your church after you hit 60. I have found that I need more reading and preparation because of this temptation to coast. My very experience in the pastorate - 45 years' worth - can actually hinder my leadership now, because sometimes I don't think there's anything left to learn. That's arrogance.

Learn to lead by listening. Once we stop listening, we stop growing. Attend growth conferences, methods seminars, theological schools and denominational conventions. Listen to educational tapes, and always listen closely when pastors who are building large churches speak. Make notes of what they say. Develop a file on church growth and organize it so you can refer to it quickly. But more than that- look for lessons in your congregation. Talk to older members about their experiences. Ask questions about their families, their jobs, their successes and failures. Treat pastoral visitation like going to school. Older people are almost never asked about themselves; they feel like no one knows them and no one cares about them. They have a wealth of experience and techniques no one has ever asked them to share. There is an extra benefit to this activity. When they tell you about themselves, they are making a personal investment in you. They will notice when you teach and preach things they have told you and follow your advice. They will become loyal to you, because you know them, and they feel they know you. (One tip on church politics: when a pastor has the older people and the little kids loving him, there's not a whole lot anyone else can do to him.)

Learn to lead by example. Set the right kind of example. Not everyone has this natural ability, but it can be developed. Set an example you want to live up to. People are motivated by example. If a pastor isn't good at motivating people, he should try to gather people around him who are motivators. He should orient the motivators to the vision, and turn them loose to excite the congregation. When the right example is set in witnessing, testifying, teaching, singing, outreach, people often respond.

Learn to lead by organizing. It takes time to reorganize each department of a church, but in the long run the leader saves time and energy by taking the initiative. Any organization is more productive when an efficient and flexible organizational plan is followed. No department or ministry can be neglected in the church's organizational plan. And everything you reorganize teaches you something about leading- either by your mistakes or by your successes.

Learn to lead by attitude. The pastor must develop a positive attitude and lead with this attitude. Before long the church will adopt this attitude. Of course, they will also adopt the pastor's sour, negative attitude, if that is what he has. The choice is entirely up to the pastor. Again, develop a public persona you want to live up to. Dedicate yourself to the picture of Christ-likeness God has chosen for you to reveal to the world.

Learn to lead by immersion and sampling. Pastors should gather ideas, plans and procedures from every available source. If another church has a productive program, take a look at it, and see what you can garner from it. No one can come up with a method himself to meet every ministry need. It takes a strong leader to revive a dying church, and no one is born with every kind of leadership ability and know-how that is necessary for this task. It must be developed, and it is up to the pastor to learn what he should do. Whatever his church is or becomes will depend on leadership.

The strong pastor must be a good preacher. Every pastor should literally "preach to pack the church" for every service. The Sunday morning service should be evangelistic, because that is usually when visitors are in services. It is inadvisable to be controversial, but it is always important to be interesting and exciting. Make sure your sermons are a production, but not just an act. Make each sermon an event people will remember. The Sunday evening sermon should be evangelistic if unsaved people attend, but if not, shift gears to preach to the needs of the congregation--doctrine, Biblical examples, and encouragement. Wednesday evenings are appropriate for addressing standards, motivation, organization and vision. Each of these services hosts a different type of congregation with unique needs.

Preaching should be positive. Every sermon should be designed to stimulate the positive emotions of the listeners. People will remember truth better if it is wrapped in a character of an event, but be careful not to use stories designed to manipulate or simply illicit an emotional response.

Messages should be designed to address congregational needs, not in what you happen to be interested in. In the early 1960s, I heard a church consultant named Wendell Nance say, "Good preachers do not get their sermons from the Bible- they get them from the congregation, and then go to the Bible to find the answers." Every sermon should be pertinent to those who are receiving it. Sermons should build people. Christ should be presented in every message. The goal of every sermon is to present Christ through a discussion of truth and exhortation to let Christ lift people in every area of their lives.

I read of a survey in which the number one reason people gave for attending their particular church was that "they liked the preacher and the preaching." This means that every pastor has the responsibility to be a good preacher. Since there are different measures of gifts, not everyone will be a great preacher; but that doesn't excuse anyone from the responsibility of being a good preacher. Preaching must be worked at and practiced. The harsh reality is that preaching is a technique. Like leadership, this technique can be developed. We don't have to worry about being manipulative if we maintain our love relationship with Christ.

Congregations are led through preaching. People are led to Christ, discipleship, deeper commitment, emotional stability, faithful stewardship, organizational stability, cooperative ministry and personal growth through preaching. Pastoral preaching is a key to growth and vitality in the church.

Vision

Churches need a holy excitement. There must be an anxious desire on the part of the congregation when meeting together. There must be an enthusiasm that goes beyond ritual and obligation. The congregation should expect big crowds at services. They should always expect God to act. They must expect people to come to the altar. They must expect God to meet their own needs.

The pastor must cast the vision. He must stay with God until he is empty of self, filled to the brim and overflowing with God's presence, and then arrive in the pulpit with God's spirit in such abundance that it spills over onto the congregation. The fire, enthusiasm, faith, the belief and positive tone of the leader who comes fresh from the altar will grip the congregation. They will take up the vision, but not until they see God's man burning with it.

Pastors may choose to preach their opinions, articulate their political philosophies, browbeat and manipulate members, or organize and train through the pulpit ministry, but it will ultimately fail without God's man spending time with God, because it does not contain God's vision for the church. The pastor is the key to bringing life to the body. Once the body of Christ catches the vision, they will reach out, evangelize and witness and the church will grow. The pastor must bring Christ (life) to the body. That is his duty.

For years I tried to push, pull, nag, and sometimes even threaten, desperately trying to motivate a congregation to be faithful to evangelistic ministries. I begged members to tithe, witness, work, and simply attend regularly. All my efforts resulted in disappointments. But when the Body received life, when the Body caught fire, when they caught the vision, they did all these things and more on their own. Whenever a church buys into the Godly pastor's vision, worship attendance grows, souls are saved, backsliders are reclaimed, and excitement blossoms, it can be said that revival has come. Valid church growth depends on getting people to see the world through God's eyes. It can be done. It must be done. And it all begins with the pastor.

"Where there is no vision the people perish." The church board and other church leaders need a vision of reaching the entire community for Christ. That isn't always the case. This vision must be developed through painstakingly patient teaching and preaching. Many church boards think only of survival, but if God's vision for lost souls is renewed within their hearts, godly men will become committed to winning their town for Jesus. Then they will commit to the entire congregation what has been committed to them.

The pastor shouldn't be the only person who understands his vision. The whole church must acquire a vision of doing great things for God. Two things are involved in this vision. It must be important, and it must be believable. The congregation must believe that reaching their whole community, at least their whole neighborhood, is important, and they must believe it is possible. This vision must contain both present and future aspects. The future vision must be both short-term and long-term. The church must have an idea of what God will do through them this year, during the next five years, and in the next ten years. The vision must begin with the pastor and be conveyed to the boards. The boards must adopt it and disseminate it to the congregation. The congregation must accept it and spread it to new members.

The church must believe that the community can be reached. The church vision must include a strategy for reaching into and evangelizing every part of society. The church must provide transportation to those who cannot get to services any other way. The church must have senior citizen ministries to address the fastest-growing segment of U.S. society. Children's ministries must be offered to communities whose children are being lost to abuse, neglect and abortion. Teen ministries that are both appropriate to the congregation and pertinent to the community must be offered. Christian schools should be provided when the public school system is hostile to Christian values. Bible studies are necessary to bring an over-informed and under-educated society into focus on Biblical truth. Visitation is necessary for meeting the needs of the lonely and disenfranchised on comfortable territory; i.e., their own homes. Anything that could work should be considered as part of the church's visionary strategy.

This vision will require organization, finances and facilities. If the vision is truly caught by the congregation, the congregation will produce these ministries on its own accord because it sees the need and the possibilities. Organizing, staffing and facilitating a church without congregational appropriation of the vision, is like pulling hen's teeth, but once the congregation appropriates the vision, they pass it on. The pastor is the one who has been delegated this task of articulating the vision. It is a grave responsibility, but God has thrust it upon him.

ROLES: THE ROLE OF THE LAY LEADER

We give thanks to God always for you all, making mention of you in our prayers; remembering without ceasing your work of faith, and labor of love, and patience of hope in our LORD Jesus Christ, in the sight of God and our Father; knowing, brethren beloved, your election of God.
1 Thessalonians 1:2-4

The world is doomed. We can't save it. Our purpose is to save people out of it through evangelism and teaching those we evangelize to live right. Jesus gave this mandate in Matthew 28:19-20. When the aggressive edge of fulfilling that mandate is taken away from a church, tragic things happen. The pastor must convince his church that this is its mandate. God's method for fulfilling His mandate is the ministry of the individual members of local congregations.

Ministry Priorities

In the Book of Acts, everyone seems to have been involved in evangelism at some level. This implies an important principle: No ministry that does not have evangelism and/or discipleship as the ultimate goal should be allowed to exist in the church. Why should a fundamental, evangelistic church involve itself in any ministry that uses its time, energy, and money, but does not result in evangelism and edification? Churches must be conscious of the God-given order to evangelize and edify. That is the church's task.

Personal Responsibility

The pastor, board members, and congregation must take the responsibility to fulfill God's Great Commission seriously. A local church can fulfill it. Every church can grow and thrive. Every church can evangelize and edify. Every pastor can be confident he is leading the charge to fulfill the task of the church. Every member can know he is a part of a church that is obeying God's word.

No pastor can do this alone. Neither can he win everyone to Christ nor be the sole motivator of the flock. These responsibilities require lay-leadership. Many church membership rolls are filled with inactive members. Congregations are often more concerned about meeting their budgets than with people meeting the Lord. Church membership is often more a matter of prestige than a challenge for service. Few members are ever challenged to be either faithful stewards or dedicated followers of Christ. Salaried staff members are expected to do all the work of the ministry.

The Imperative of Enlistment

Lay leaders are a vital part of the local church. They can be a resource for its revival, but they may also be its cause of death. Entrenched lay leaders who fear they will lose their power, and frantically try to retain it are hazards to a church. On the other hand, if they are built up in the faith, taught to pray, gain victory over temptation, and obtain knowledge of the Bible, they can be the difference between life and death for the church. Building up the membership in the faith, however, must be intentional. It doesn't just happen. The pastor must actively, purposefully, and conscientiously choose to build up lay leaders, and it is vital that he carefully choose which lay leaders to build up. That's the important thought process: lay leaders must be chosen, and they must be chosen carefully, with the future of the church in view.

Preparation for Service

Wherever a growing, thriving, fundamental church is found, active and equipped lay leaders will be found as well. A breakdown occurs when people are active but not trained well. They either get frustrated and burn out, or content themselves with doing a second-class job. Many pastors have had the sad task of trying to work with lay leaders who do not want to serve God or his church, but have been elected or appointed anyway. They may hold onto the office because they are too embarrassed to resign, or simply as a means of controlling the church and its finances, or to keep control from the pastor or some other layman. These situations are often due to the fact they were improperly discipled to serve in the first place.

It is obvious that there is a need for initial preparation of the laymen for leadership roles. A layman must not be allowed to assume a leadership position he has the wrong concept of, attitude toward, or training for. A person with a poor spiritual condition will not be improved by an appointment to a leadership condition. The man of God must pour himself into the lay leader. Loyalty to the pastor and a grasp of church growth concepts should develop in a layman as he is equipped for service.

Caring for Lay Leaders

Lay leaders don't just happen-they must be developed. The pastor must select leaders prayerfully and train them carefully. Once they are chosen and developed, once they have performed their assigned duties conscientiously, the church must honor and praise them. The pastor must trust them and allow them to develop their own leadership abilities. They must not see themselves as rubber stamps or puppets, but as men and women who have an opinion the pastor and church will prayerfully consider. They must see themselves as important servants fulfilling church needs, helping the church grow and evangelize.

The pastor should honor his board members publicly in the services. Board members should know they are important. They hold honorable positions, but they will lose that position if they do not function honorably. If the pastor cooperates with the board, they will usually cooperate with him.

Delegation

The successful pastor must delegate responsibility. Churches die when pastors refuse to delegate, do not know how to delegate, or do not get positive responses from those to whom responsibilities are delegated.

There are at least two groups to whom the pastor must learn to delegate. The first group is volunteers, those people who, out of love for Christ and his church, give voluntarily of their time and energy to minister. These people may serve as department superintendents, teachers, musicians, deacons, trustees, ushers and secretaries. The second group is the paid staff, specialists who manage programs and provide leadership in specific ministries.

Some pastors have never learned that it is better to have ten people doing the work than to have one man doing the work of ten people. The pastor who has to be the ramrod in every program and be intimately involved in every minute detail of the church program is kidding himself. He will reach a breaking point where neither he nor the church can grow any further.

Accountability

The ideal situation, which can and must be obtained if a church is to continue growing, is for the pastor to delegate responsibility, and then call for an accounting from those in charge. For example, the pastor may appoint a head usher. He then teaches and trains that person about the requirements for the head usher. The two of them will appoint the ushering committee, and then the head usher takes charge. He trains the ushers committee, delegates their positions, and details their work. He then provides periodic reports to the pastor. The pastor will also give additional direction to the head usher, who in turn will see that those directions are carried out.

After choosing leaders, they must be trained. The classic outline for teaching skills has four steps: demonstration (I do it and you watch), participation (I do it and you do it, too), observation (You do it and I watch), and delegation (You do it, and I do something else). This model will work with every ministry of the church. Instead of one person running himself ragged, handling every problem and putting out every wildfire, there can be ten or twelve people in charge. This means that pastor can multiply his ministry twelve-fold.

It is not uncommon to see pastors running Christian schools offered through their churches in spite of the fact that the school has hired a principal. He micro-manages the music

program, visitation, and the Sunday school. In fact, he runs everything. The common and very appropriate term for this is "control freak."

Obviously, a church can't turn over a ministry to someone without his or her measuring effectiveness. There must be intelligent delegation of responsibility and there must also be intelligent accountability. Weekly, monthly and quarterly updates should be required from department heads. When the pastor is displeased with the outcomes in a particular department, he must have the courage and authority to tell the department leader about his dissatisfaction. It is probably easier to deal with paid staff than with volunteer staff, but both must be held accountable. Both love and firmness are required if church programs are to progress effectively.

One way of making accountability less of a "top-down" activity is public recognition. When someone is appointed to a position, it should be announced to the whole congregation in a public setting. The pastor should describe to the whole church what the appointee is tasked with doing. The whole job should be described, and the person should be asked to stand up so the church can applaud for him. The pastor should tell the congregation that they are responsible for supporting the appointee, and how serious the job is. That way, when a person doesn't do the job, the whole church knows what's going on (or what's not going on). Also, the pastor isn't stuck with being the bad guy when someone isn't performing up to expectations. The whole church is in on the appointment, and the whole church is in on the evaluation.

Qualifications

When choosing volunteer leaders, the pastor should always select on the basis of known ability to perform specific required tasks, plus people skills. Some people can work and accomplish much, but can never get along with others. These persons should never be appointed to leadership positions. Leaders should be chosen on the basis of faithfulness. Are they dependable? Are they task-oriented? Are they cooperative?

When hiring paid staff members, one rule must hold: all staff members are hired, and can be fired, by the pastor. Their loyalty must be to the pastor. He must be sure of this before hiring them, and he must work hard to keep their loyalty (i.e., he must be worthy of their loyalty because of his behavior, not his position). They should be hired on the basis of ability. Some churches hire a second man because he is a good preacher or popular. The pastor should decide what areas need help. What type of person would be the best fit? Who can do this job the way it needs to be done?

Leaders must be chosen carefully, prayerfully and deliberately. They must be trained, placed in a suitable position, authorized for service, and held accountable for their performance. Delegation and accountability are requirements for a growing church.

If the pastor finds that a staff member can't be trusted or is a bad fit or is simply incompetent, he must take time getting rid of him. Anyone who serves in a pastoral position gathers supporters after a while. An abrupt firing will turn those supporters against the leadership-especially the pastor. It is more important to take your time and give the person counsel and every opportunity to straighten up or gain competence. When the supporters see that the pastor is supportive of the person but he still isn't loyal, or still doesn't fit in or still can't perform the required duties, they will appreciate the pastor's integrity and become his supporters.

Always remember: after you've disciplined or dismissed a staff member, even if the congregation appreciates your willingness to take a stand, there will then be a question in their minds from that time on over how you will handle them if they mess up. If the congregation sees you handle an errant member with grace and patience, they will trust you as a leader, pastor and manager. If they begin to perceive you as ruthless, they may be tempted to launch a pre-emptive strike when they make mistakes.

There is nothing more important to a church than choosing the right members to be in charge of different areas of ministry. Pastors never make any decisions more important than the delegation of responsibility for church ministries.

PART THREE

Strategies

Hope is not a plan. Building God's church is not a matter of "Let go and led God." Pastors are called to lead. The word leadership implies that you know where you're going. This section deals with particular steps the pastoral leader might take to turn around a dying church.

STRATEGIES:
PLANTING THE SEEDS OF REVIVAL

I have planted, Apollos watered; but God gave the increase. So then neither is he that planteth anything, neither he that watereth; but God that giveth the increase.

Now he that planteth and he that watereth are one: and every man shall receive his own reward according to his own labor.

For we are laborers together with God: ye are God's husbandry...
--1 Corinthians 3:6-9

I am often asked what I would do if I were to move to another church to be the pastor. How would I go about reviving a church and getting it started on the road to growth? Would I do the same things I did at the other churches I pastored?

Well, I have to confess- I tried every time to do what I had done at the last church I had pastored. Being from Missouri, I have a naturally conservative tendency to stick to the tried and true (it is the "Show-Me State," after all). Actually, a few things worked every time. But, sooner or later, I had to assess the situation, including my own attitude, and make some adjustments. After all, if you're going to plant a crop, you have to be conscious of the climate. Understanding your own climate, and the climate of your congregation, and especially the climate of your field of service, are necessary before planting any seeds.

Self-examination

It is always possible that somewhere down the road God will call a pastor to another field of service. In fact, if a minister has been successful, it is more than likely that another congregation will try to hire him away. No minister can be sure he can transplant the same degree of growth and prosperity he has experienced in his present pastorate to his next. I do think about it quite often, and each time I get excited at the prospect of once again seeing the Lord work his miraculous changes in another congregation.

I was recently talking to a minister who has a part in a mission work in the Philippines. He was bubbling over with excitement, and could hardly wait to tell me about all God is doing in that place. Everyone should be that excited about God's call on his life. With that in mind, and with the knowledge that one day God might call me to revive another work, I am now ready to attempt to answer the question posed earlier in this chapter.

As I write this, I am preaching a series of revival services in Nebraska. I must confess that this revival has challenged me to consider whether or not the Lord might once again move me out into a new field of service. There was a time when I actually thought I would never want to take an established church and attempt to create a climate where God's spirit could bring revival, but those days are long gone. I actually get more excited today over the prospects of reviving a dying church than at the prospects of starting a new church.

Perspectives

It is again necessary to refer to our definition of a dying church. A dying church is a church that is not growing. Any church that is not growing is in the process of dying. It may not be dead, and in fact may never die completely; but if it isn't growing it is in the process of dying.

We must also understand that the "reviving" is the work of the Lord. No preacher can revive a church any more than any preacher can revive a backslidden Christian. However, God does bless the methods of his man as he sets out to do God's will in a church. Bear in mind that the contents of this book do not mean that I think I can revive a dying church. This work simply records a program that has been blessed by God.

We must also understand that not all successes are necessarily equal. My present pastorate has grown far more than all my previous pastorates, but all have grown. Who knows what would have happened if I had known to do the things in my previous pastorates that I have done here? Actually, the successes I experienced at other churches might be more or less than I am now experiencing if I had done there what I have done in my present pastorate. The point is that if my heart is right with God, and he has called me to a place of service, and I institute a program similar to the one I outline in this work, there will be some degree of success.

Denominationalism

Many church growth experts agree that any time a congregation of blood-washed Christians is determined to grow for Christ, it can do it. Any church can grow if the congregation wants to grow and is willing to pay the price. God's people can do anything they really want to do. The leader has the responsibility to provoke this desire.

Some pastors have the idea that denominational churches cannot grow, which is not true. Some even believe that denominations are somewhat demonic, which is also false. Others think that if a church and pastor believe in, pray for, cooperate with and support a denomination, they are nothing more than puppets being manipulated and brainwashed by the denominational hierarchy. That may be true of some denominations and with some pastors, but it is certainly not true of all denominations, and it is not true of me. I am a lifelong member of a denomination, one that I love very much. I support it and cooperate with it in order to help send out missionaries, train ministers and other Christian workers, provide a place for young preachers to pastor, fellowship and gain unity with other men and women of God who hold similar doctrinal distinctions.

The local church cooperating in a denomination is stronger, has a greater worldwide ministry, and has more to offer its members, than does the church that cuts itself off from all ties with other churches. Affiliation with a denominational church doesn't diminish God's blessings for that congregation, so long as the denomination is fundamental, evangelistic, evangelical, and Godly.

As a member of a denomination I have learned that I must be loyal if I am to be obedient to Scripture. Loyalty requires me to be vigilant to keep my denomination free from social liberalism, moral worldliness, theological impurity, and witch-hunters. I believe, from experience, that maintaining ties to a denomination has no bearing on whether or not my church will grow. Growth is strictly between God and the individual church.

A Common Mistake

As leader, the pastor is responsible for stirring up the congregation's desire to grow. That cannot be accomplished without changing congregational attitudes. Scripture teaches that the mind determines reality. "As a man thinketh in his heart in his heart, so is he" (Proverbs 23:7).

For example, suppose a minister accepts a pastorate and initiates a program of organization and development designed to produce growth. The congregation likes him because he's new, and his message and delivery are a little different from what they are used to, so they accept his changes. They attend services faithfully, tithe, volunteer for different ministries, participate in visitation, and even vote to build new facilities.

But time passes and the honeymoon ends. People begin to balk in their participation and support. They have been doing things they don't understand. They don't know why they have been promoting or visiting or even building, so they stop. At that point the pastor has a decision to make: either press on alone, or gather a few loyalists to help. Pastors in this very common situation often end up picking fights and become bitter, or else they leave the congregation for another field.

What happened? And why is that such a common scenario? Why do most pastors only spend two or three years at a pastorate, and then leave? The reason may be negligence of a few simple rules for church growth, originally articulated by Donald McGavran, which I mentioned previously:

- Churches that believe growth is God's will grow, and churches that don't believe growth is God's will don't grow.
- Churches that pray for growth grow, and churches that don't pray for growth don't grow.

- Churches that know what produces growth grow, and churches that don't know what produces growth don't grow; and
- Churches that do what produces growth grow, and churches that don't do what produces growth don't grow.

Those are the rules. The pastor in our illustration skipped rules one, two and three, and went directly to four: change and activity. Faith, knowledge and prayer were ignored.

Most pastors have to admit that this is the mistake we all make. We attempt to build a house without a foundation. When we accept a pastorate, the needs are evident to us, so, instead of observing rules one, two and three, we go directly to rule four. Members don't understand, believe in, or have spiritual convictions about the things they've been doing, so they quit. We get frustrated, so, after beating our heads against the wall, we quit. If we never learn to obey these rules, we repeat the same mistake over and over. As a result, our pastorates are usually short and not so sweet. We are oblivious to the people we hurt, the ethics we ignore, and the methods we use. The people initially follow us out of respect and love, but when the honeymoon ends, so does their loyalty. There must be a better way.

The Right Steps in the Right Order

There is! As surely as one comes before two and three before four, rules one, two, and three precede rule four. The wise pastor will observe the rules in their proper order.

Jim McAlister
REVIVING A DYING CHURCH

Since the first rule is Churches that believe growth is God's will grow, the first and most logical move for the new pastor is to convince his new congregation that growth is God's will. That is neither as easy as it sounds nor as difficult as might be feared. It is simply a job that must be done. The pastor should systematically teach the congregation that, since growth is God's will, non- growth must be sin. Once taught, this must be constantly reinforced. The key is to let this word fall like gentle rain in sermons, lessons, prayer, and private conversation, always softly teaching and convincing people that "growth is God's will and non-growth is sin." This may take months or it may take years, but it is better to build on a foundation than to build on the sand.

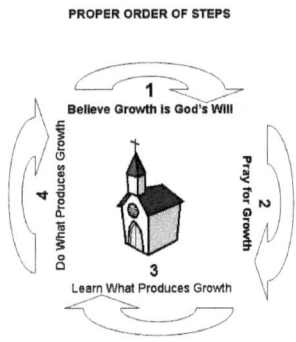

Everything that is alive was created to grow. Nothing begins dying until it stops growing. The congregation must be convinced that growth is God's mandate to the church. They must see growth as a command, not a choice.

The evidence that your teaching and preaching are accomplishing their goal is that a new concern for the church, numbers, souls, and growth will appear. People will begin approaching the pastor with some unusual requests, such as "Teach us to win souls," or "Let's start a visitation program," or "Shouldn't we reorganize our Sunday school?" When these requests begin, the congregation is ready to move on to rule two: Churches that pray for growth grow.

At that point, it should not be too difficult to encourage a congregation to pray for church growth. It is said that two seminary students visited Charles Spurgeon's Metropolitan Church in London. A kindly man met them at the door before services began and asked, "Would you like to see our heat plant?" They had no interest in the "heat plant" but didn't want to offend the gentleman. He took them to the basement and opened the door to reveal 700 saints kneeling in prayer. "This is our heat plant. These saints pray for our services and heat up the church." Then the gentleman introduced himself as Charles Spurgeon.

It is essential that churches pray for growth. Our Lord said, "Pray the Lord of the harvest to thrust forth laborers into the harvest" (Matthew 9:38). We need to obey his orders and pray in a way that only we pastors can. The congregation must be taught to pray as a church and led to pray by their leaders. Lasting growth comes as a result of a convinced church asking the Lord of the harvest to help them fit into His plan for growth. A church needs to maintain a specific prayer list for the lost, for church unity, for Holy Spirit power, and for church growth.

When the pastor begins to hear several members praying for church growth, he knows he is now ready to move to the third phase: Churches that know what produces growth grow. The congregation is ready for training. There is no need to offer training until the congregation is convinced of the necessity of church growth and is praying for church growth. Ushers, deacons, trustees, financial officers, teachers, musicians, soul-winners classes, altar workers and follow-up disciples all need training. Job descriptions should be drawn up for each position, approved by the board, and used for recruitment. People who volunteer for ministry deserve a clear picture of whatever they happen to be volunteering for.

Once the training, based on prayer and theological conviction, is in place, the congregation is ready to start changing the church program. Churches that do what produces growth grow. This doesn't mean we should wait until phase four to win souls, any more than we should wait until phase three to train. In fact, an organized training program should be preceded by the informal, individual training we have been doing all along. It doesn't mean we should wait until phase two to pray. "Men ought always to pray and not to faint" (Luke 18:1). It does mean we must create a desire for change in our people before making big changes, and we must educate them before instituting programs that require wholesale membership involvement.

To do that, we preach sermons on growth to convince the church of God's mandate for growth that can be found in Biblical theology. Then we provoke the church to pray for growth with our own prayer life. Then we train the congregation to do things consistent with our theology and our prayers. And finally, we get the body of Christ involved in growth activities.

These things can, and should be, exciting to any pastor. Just think- this process can be the means of bringing growth, revival, and excitement to a church that others have written off. I hope several other pastors will put this process to the test.

STRATEGIES:
PROGRAMMING FOR REVIVAL

Then said I unto them, Ye see the distress that we are in, how Jerusalem lieth waste, and the gates thereof are burned with fire; come, and let us build up the wall of Jerusalem that we be no more a reproach.

Then I told them of the hand of my God which was good upon me; as also the king's words that he had spoken unto me.

And they said, Let us rise up and build. So they strengthened their hands for this good work. --Nehemiah 2:17-18

I assumed pastorate of a church in a small town in Missouri. On the previous Sunday the church had 125 in attendance in Sunday school. The offering was $600. The church was in good shape so far as finances were concerned. There was no disunity. It had a very good pastor for the past four years and things were in fine shape. However, according to the description provided in previous chapters, it was a dying church. This church was atrophied. It might never have completely died, but it would have continued its decline if things had continued as they were.

Incrementalism

Before accepting the pastorate, I had drawn up a list of actions and changes I would make if elected pastor. The church elected me and I assumed the pastorate with the understanding that these things would be accepted.

Patience was necessary. No pastor can come into a church and change everything overnight. Incrementalism is the key to lasting change. Changes should be made so gradually that no one feels threatened. They may not even notice changes have been made until, one day, they realize that some significant improvements have been made in their situation. This process takes patience, lots of it, along with a very secure ego.

Strategies

- My first step was preparation for and formulation and communication of a church-wide program of change. The program was clearly grounded in my mind, and clearly articulated through Bible-based messages. At first the vision was mine. The next necessary step was transplantation to the minds of the people. This was accomplished through the preaching ministry. Week after week sermons were delivered on motivation, confidence, assurance, and methodology. It was also talked up to anyone who would listen, over coffee, in board meetings, in church conferences. The philosophy for the church, at first a seed in my mind, began taking root in the people's mind. The key to success in this situation was patience.

- The second step was proving by example that the new vision would work. I began visiting members, knocking on the doors of prospective attendees, witnessing and winning people to Christ. Before long, every service saw a person I had won to Christ coming forward to make a public profession. It became common, and then became expected to see people coming to the altar during services. The altars, which had been barren and tearless for so long, caught fire. Soon church members began to move to the altars in commitment and rededication. The flicker of a fire was starting in the heart of the congregation. Since everything was supported by the example of the pastor, the people did not rebel. On the contrary, they began to respond.

- The third step was to challenge the church's concept of adequate attendance. We used two motivational efforts to challenge this concept. Another church similar in size to ours was challenged for a fall attendance contest. The losing pastor would travel to the winner's church, preach a message, and shine the winner's shoes in front of the congregation. The challenged pastor was a close personal friend, and very witty. He could be expected to make the shoe-shining episode enjoyable for the observing congregation, whether he was shining shoes or having his shoes shined. The church I pastored won by five people over a four-week period. This produced a lot of enthusiasm and good-natured confidence in the congregation's ability to break barriers. We next addressed the most depressing service in our whole program- the poorly attended Wednesday evening prayer service. We challenged the congregation to increase prayer meeting attendance from twelve each week to a full house for all prayer services in the near future. It took some time and a lot of effort, but within a few years we had changed the Wednesday night service from tedium to an event, with a program for each age group and a vital prayer ministry.

- The fourth strategy was providing two annual motivational/evangelistic campaigns. Evangelists who had engaging and exciting preaching styles were scheduled for spring and fall revivals every year. The evangelist, usually a pastor, would be one whose congregation was a little larger than our church. The challenge in this was a learning curve. In sports, or when learning to play a musical instrument, the student never learns from someone at a lower level of expertise than him/herself. In fact, the player's game will decline, and the musician's proficiency will become dull if he or she only participates with players or musicians at or beneath his or her level. But a better player or musician provides an edge to the experience, and motivates the student to keep up, and, therefore, improve. Evangelists were chosen according to their particular skills, strengths and expertise. One evangelist would be a motivator, while the next speaker would be a great soul winner, and the next evangelist might be a church builder. A lot of promotion and excitement were invested into every meeting. We expected a measure of success from every revival. Pre-revival weeks of prayer and promotion, and days of fasting and prayer all helped to ensure success.

- Fifth, the worship services were reorganized and accentuated. The ushers were reappointed and reorganized. They were taught that their function was to assist the pastor. Usher manuals were purchased and training classes were conducted. Then the music program was revamped. The music director was authorized to take charge and was given specific instructions concerning type and quality of music program that was expected. He was to select all the music to be performed, select choir members, and appoint musicians and special music performers. The program was improved considerably, and almost immediately, when strong leadership was provided. The changes enabled the entire worship services to support an evangelism-focused church ministry.

- The sixth step was critical for the purpose of consolidating our evangelistic and discipleship efforts: Altar workers were trained, and only those that took training were allowed to deal with those coming to the altar. An assistant pastor was added to manage and train the altar workers and to take leadership in the follow-up and visitation. A one-on-one follow-up program was initiated. I trained the second man in this ministry, and he, in turn, trained other dedicated, loyal workers to assist in teaching follow-up. A ten-lesson program was used, which required that each week the follow-up worker went to the new convert's home to ground him in the word and establish him in his faith.

- Seventh, a visitation program was launched incrementally. At first the program was informal and spontaneous, but after a year it became an organized weekly program. The assistant pastor was put in charge, consolidating it with altar work and follow-up into a full evangelism-discipleship process, and he received full cooperation and assistance from the pastor. The keys to its success were fellowship (refreshments were provided for the visitation personnel when they arrived at the church), spirituality (a brief devotion and prayer led each visitation meeting), organization (tracts and visitation assignments were provided for each visitation worker), support (workers were paired up appropriately and sent out) and encouragement/accountability (workers were required to return by 9:00 p.m. to deliver their reports).

The Sunday school was reorganized to support the program I planned. The board and the church approved this reorganization. The church adopted a graded, departmentalized organizational plan for the Sunday school. All superintendents were husband-wife teams. Men taught all boys and women taught all girls. Men taught adult classes.

The bus ministry was upgraded. At that time, it consisted of two busses and twenty-five riders. As soon as possible a bus minister was hired and additional busses were purchased.

A budget was established to sufficiently fund every department in the program. The bus ministry, music department, Sunday school and youth ministry each had a spot in the budget.

Preaching was needs oriented. Churches go through identifiable cycles, and the preaching was programmed to meet the need of the church at each phase. I found that the preaching determined the length of each phase. After I had been at the church for six years, I could check records and predict which phase of the cycle was coming up. I could then begin preaching sermons aimed at preparing for the phase. If it was a phase of lackluster performance and interest, I preached sermons calculated to affect the length of the phase. For example, December was a problem month each year. The church was a blue-collar congregation, and December often saw sudden lay-offs. Missouri winters are usually bitterly cold, and the weather can include fog, rain, snow, ice or all four. Bad attitudes and depression would settle in. Knowing this, I began preaching sermons on attitudes and faith in November. By the time December arrived, the people had been "spiritually inoculated" against depression, and the church usually managed to avoid the problem of bad attitudes. There is no substitute for knowing the cycles of the church and planning for it.

The church was continually re-organized to enable it to continue its growth and to avoid stagnation. Provisions were made for adding deacons and trustees. The church authorized the pastor and Sunday school superintendent to add classes and departments and appoint teachers. Training programs were established to assist the ministries of deacons, trustees, teachers, musicians, choir members and bus workers.

- Eighth, church growth methodology was taught to the congregation, but not until the congregation was convinced growth was God's will and non-growth was a sin. The church was constantly encouraged to pray for growth, and began to follow its leaders in doing things that produced growth. The church began to develop confidence in its capacity to accomplish great things for God. The members became pleased to tell others about their church, and were proud to invite their friends to hear their preacher, their choir and their teachers. The philosophy, program and plans of the pastor became those of the congregation. They helped him solve problems and prevent the same problems from recurring.

The results of this incremental reconstruction and reorganization were truly astounding. Seven years later Sunday school attendance averaged almost 650. The weekly income Increased greatly. Sunday evening attendance was almost 375, and Wednesday night attendance approached 325. In that year, 180 people were baptized and 173 joined the church. There were more than 300 altar decisions. The church staff had grown to 6 and a Christian school had been added.

Conditions

A dying church can be revived, but there are definitely some conditions that must be met. The pastor, and then the church, must recognize that the church is dying. An incremental plan must be initiated to revive the church. Reorganization is a requirement. The preaching will have to change to meet congregational needs. The pastor must delegate responsibility. Worship services must become attractive and encouraging experiences for the parishioners. The church's doctrine must be adhered to, and no variations can be tolerated. Worship services must focus on particular needs at the same time they are oriented to and designed for evangelism.

Organization

Reorganization is necessary if a dying church is going to be revived and resume growth, but too many churches are simply not willing to make the changes. Plenty of churches probably want to grow, but refuse to reorganize. One church had the right location (at the crossroads of two interstate highways in a large metropolitan area), the right facilities (an auditorium seating more than 600 with equal educational space and room for adequate parking), quality people available for leadership (talented, educated and of Christian character) and a talented and dedicated pastor. Unfortunately, the organizational structure prevented growth. When approached about reorganization, the pastor simply shrugged and passed the idea off as unimportant.

Even if a church is organized and functioning properly, it won't stay that way long, because new people bring new challenges, needs change as members grow older and growth demands flexible administrative structures. When one compares Moses' leadership of the children of Israel with New Testament apostles, several similarities are detected:

- The leaders established priorities.
- They chose qualified men and delegated responsibility to them.
- They organized for the particular needs they were facing at the time.
- Their organization and structures were flexible. They were not afraid to change as required.

Obviously, no program, organization or structure can be set in stone. Leaders must continuously organize, reorganize, and reorganize again as the situation demands it. Every area of a church must be regularly evaluated to identify the

organizational changes that are needed to fit the current ministry needs of the church, and its purposes for existence: evangelization and discipleship.

Churches reach plateaus. At each plateau some phase of the church's structure needs adjustment. Any pastor who insists that his church can continue to function and grow with an outmoded organizational model will soon discover that he has made a foolish mistake. Any congregation that refuses to change to fit needs will find itself at a dead end sooner or later.

For example, a Sunday school will not function for 500 students the same way it did for 200. Ushers cannot serve 600 congregants the way they served 300. Promotional methods for a church of 700 members must be upgraded or replaced before meeting the needs of 1000.

Organization begins in the mind and heart of the pastor. Every pastor should ask some important questions: Where do I begin? How much time do I have? What are my expectations? Are those expectations realistic? What is expected from me? Are those expectations realistic? What are the basic assets needed to do the job? Where does success really lie? What tools do I need? What are the signs of control? What are my goals? Am I ready and willing to make changes in myself and in my church? Is the congregation ready and willing to make necessary changes?

Organization will only be effective when the congregation is convinced that it is necessary. One pastor heard a Sunday school expert speak about reorganization and structure at a conference, and got very excited about what he heard. He went back to his church and tore out all the walls in his educational building to reorganize his Sunday school program. He later had to rebuild the walls when the congregation rebuked him for making physical changes without church approval. Another pastor simply added more workers to the organization without demonstrating the need for them. Both of these men could have avoided a great deal of embarrassment and frustration (not to mention sweat) by preparing their churches for change and getting input from the leadership.

Any observant pastor should be able to sense a need for change in the organization and program of the church. When a couple adds a child to their family, they know they will need more room and a different living arrangement, not to mention a different lifestyle. Average churches remain average because they do not respond to obvious needs. Divine guidance isn't necessary if pastors depend on wisdom, which God gives to anyone who asks. Many organizational needs are obvious to the objective observer. A lot of thinking and planning is necessary before a pastor can decide what should be done.

Organization is part of God's Plan. People are won with evangelism and kept with organization. Organization is Biblical. God had an organized program for creation. Each day he built on the previous day's work. God had an organized plan for preserving the race in Noah's day, providing the food supply in Joseph's day, in the birth of His Son, and the feeding of the 5,000, and God certainly has an organized plan for His church. It is within God's will for church leadership to develop and maintain an organizational plan.

Organization is necessary for effectiveness. If you are a naturally talented person, a genius, a charismatic personality who can do whatever needs to be done in an expert manner on the spot, you don't need any organization. But let's assume that you're just a normal pastor, like me. I have a rule that I have, unfortunately, broken more than I'd like to admit. Here it is: Anything that is done well consistently is practiced and/or prepared for in advance. Whenever I break this rule, I usually wander into uncharted territory and experience a lot of stress. I say usually, because sometimes it works out, but when that happens, I really think I'm obeying the rule, because I have prepared enough, at least spiritually, in advance of the task. Anything that is consistently done well in your church will be practiced and/or prepared for in advance. Here are some critical areas needing organization (practice and preparation).

Organize the music program. The importance of music to the revitalization of a church cannot be overestimated. The music program is supposed to usher the pastor into the pulpit. It lays the groundwork for the sermon. It lifts the congregation's hearts to the Lord in worship, making them open to His guidance through the ministry of the Word. It doesn't automatically mean that spiritual revival will take place, but music certainly influences the spiritual life of any congregation. At the very least, the music of a church must be programmed. A director should be appointed over music planning, organizing a choir and the development of a special music program, and accumulating a library of music. A worship committee is also helpful to these efforts. A monthly schedule for special music is necessary for cohesive worship services.

Organize church governing boards, such as deacons or elders, trustees, Christian education, etc. A policy that provides for a rotating board member structure works well. Such a plan recognizes that small churches have a small pool from which to choose board members by avoiding the dead end of "term limits," but also restricts a single person's ability to dominate a board indefinitely. Board power must be equalized. Deacons and Trustees should have equal authority. Job descriptions should be developed and approved for each board position. Since nearly all churches maintain boards and these boards have definite power and can determine the future of the church, it is reasonable that they should be properly organized.

Organize church finances. People who refuse to tithe or know nothing about finance shouldn't control Church finance. A stewardship committee should be organized to handle the financial needs of a church. Job descriptions for positions on this committee should specify tithing and financial management experience as qualifications for service. This committee should be appointed by and serve at the pleasure of the pastor.

Organize the Outreach Program. Visitation programs probably require more training, encouragement, and pastoral participation than any other ministry, because evangelism is intimidating to many Christians, and can be frustrating and exhausting to those who aren't intimidated. Satan doesn't want it to happen, and uses fear and time pressure to prevent participation. For these reasons, visitation workers seem to become more irritated than other ministry workers when the program is disorganized. It is essential that a regular time and day for visitation be established, and that the program starts on time. Visitation workers should gather together before leaving on visits to receive assignments, refreshments, hear a short devotion, and be teamed up with a partner for the evening. Make sure everyone visits prospects appropriate to the age, gender and ministry interest of the visitor. Everyone should report back to the church by 9:00 p.m. for personal sharing and encouragement. Accurate records must be kept of visits, and should be prayerfully reviewed by the evangelism director on a weekly basis.

If you have a bus Ministry, then don't take it lightly. Nothing that requires so much money for fuel and vehicles and insurance, so much dedication from drivers, and so much cooperation from children's workers cannot be afforded to be disregarded. Organization spells the difference between success and failure in this ministry. A bus ministry doesn't just happen- preparation is essential.

Before leading a church into a bus ministry, the pastor must calculate the initial costs of the busses, painting, lettering, general upkeep, promotional costs, maintenance, bookkeeping costs, and man-hours on the street. Although this runs into much money, it pays huge spiritual dividends. A bus ministry is worthwhile if a congregation's priorities are appropriate. If the salvation of lost people is the most earnest desire, then the bus ministry pays.

Care must be exercised that a church not gets top-heavy in this ministry. The bus rider population is generally an unstable crowd compared to the drive-in crowd. Since this ministry is almost always centered on children, unless the church makes the effort to focus on bus parents, it will produce few leaders and no tithers in the short run. A church that allows the bus ministry to occupy the lion's share of its attendance will have few workers to care for the bus riders when they come.

Bad feelings can develop between the drive-in members and the bus riders. A second-class citizenship cannot be allowed to develop between bus riders and drive-in members. For a while, "bus" kids had a negative connotation in our congregation, and some teachers complained about having them in their classes. Since we were really short on space for children's church and Sunday school at that time, we developed a separate program to teach our bus children "how they ought to behave themselves in the house of God." We called it Commuter Church (removing the "bus kid" stigma), a program that combined Sunday school and worship into one service, and held it in the main sanctuary during the Sunday school hour. Children "graduated" from this program into the regular Sunday school and Children's Church, based on the director's recommendation. We did that for two years, until we remodeled our educational building and got more teachers. By then, the stigma, too, had "graduated" out, and the issue disappeared. Remember one of our operating principles: time is the pastor's best friend. People have limited attention spans and faulty memories. If it is out of their sight, it truly does go out of their minds.

Sunday school and children's church workers must be prepared to deal with children who will have limited knowledge of the Bible and may have few social graces. You never run out of unruly kids. We reached a large number of junior high kids last year, and some behavioral problems developed in the worship services. So, we started a special program for junior high kids called "C.I.A." (Christ In All), which preaches salvation and teaches manners. An ex-MP from the Navy and a junior high teacher (two real toughies) developed the program, and the students "graduate" into worship services on their recommendation.

The bus ministry cannot be allowed to develop into a stand-alone ministry, an end unto itself. It is important to use the bus ministry as a feeder into homes, to try to win the bus parents. If the parents are not reached, the children will eventually be lost. It is probably advisable to send different visitors to see the bus parents, someone other than the usual bus worker.

Church facilities must be evaluated to ensure that there is adequate space for Sunday school and children's church. You have to have somewhere to put the kids you bring in, and it can't be a dump. Unsaved people are not obligated to "understand" that the church doesn't have a lot of money.

Unsaved people view the church as just another service provider, and therefore churches are in competition with malls, schools, and amusement parks.

Bus workers must be recruited continually and trained in methods and the philosophy of the bus ministry. Bus ministries tend to have a high turnover rate because of the large amount of time that must be dedicated to the ministry. This may be minimized by providing adequate staffing for each bus (captain, runner, driver, and secretary), rotating drivers, and arranging for captains and workers to be off one weekend per month if they so desire.

Neighborhoods must be targeted and canvassed to ascertain the number of un-churched children in each. Target areas should be divided into routes. Several "super" promotions should be conducted during the first month of the bus ministry to encourage riders to become regulars. Several enlistment teams should be prepared to go out all day on Saturdays during the first month, with two people per team. Attractive brochures with church name and schedule of services should be distributed. Each survey team should be assigned specific areas for canvassing. Someone experienced in database management must record all available information concerning prospects. The system that is developed with this information will be used to keep track of visits, attendance, address changes, moves, etc.

Keep the workers in the loop. Conduct a bus workers meeting each Saturday morning prior to visitation time. Provide refreshments, fellowship, devotion, promotional material, and handouts. The bus workers should visit all riders and make prospect calls weekly.

An appointed time must be set for workers to meet back at the church for snacks and an excitement report. This way, networking among workers can begin to solve problems on routes, referrals can be traded back and forth, and workers who had an unproductive day will receive reassurance from those whose visits were very productive. Mutual encouragement is the key for maintaining any type of outreach program. Before long the discouraged will become encouragers.

Busses must be ready to go on Sunday morning, full of fuel, ready with a driver, and preventive maintenance already done. Busses must be kept clean, painted, and in good running order, and should be checked weekly. In the winter, the busses should be warmed up long before departure time. Someone other than the bus captain should take care of the mechanical needs.

Promotions (or "gimmicks") provide some legitimate opportunity for criticism of the bus ministry. Some complain that bubble gum and gifts for bus kids are manipulative. These same critics usually have no ethical problem when special singing groups are scheduled for the adult worship services. Such criticisms are really illogical. Is it rational to believe that kids in the 21st century will continuously ride to church on a cold, uncomfortable bus for a piece of gum?

Another problem is the ride home. The kids have been gone from home possibly three hours or more. They may be tired and anxious to get back. They shouldn't be allowed to just sit on the bus with nothing to do. If that happens, they will get bored and concoct ways to entertain themselves, which almost always gets them into trouble. Keep them busy on the bus singing choruses, having Bible quizzes, reviewing their Sunday school lessons or playing games. In other words, entertain them. They won't fight if they are occupied.

The biggest problem with the bus ministry is spiritual warfare. The devil hates it. He will attack the bus ministry because it reaches those usually ignored by churches. Workers and riders will quit because they've lost their zeal. The busses will break down. Workers will get mad at riders and other workers, and so will riders. None of these problems are beyond solutions, as long as the pastor and bus director keep warm hearts, sweet spirits and good attitudes. No one on the staff, in the membership or among the ridership should be allowed to develop self-righteous spirits. Organize a group of dedicated prayer warriors for each bus route. Feed them all pertinent information concerning their routes.

A bus ministry can revitalize a church. Hundreds can be led to Christ through an evangelistic transportation ministry. Great growth can be realized if the congregation's organization is maintained. It pays to organize. A successful pastor believes in and practices the biblical concept of organization in the church.

This material doesn't come close to covering all the areas of a church that need organization, but I believe these things are very important. Once a pastor gets used to organizing, spotting problems before they arise, building programs incrementally, and thinking proactively rather than reactively, he will probably be able to administer the needs of a revived church adequately. At the very least, he will know what he doesn't know, and hire people who do know.

STRATEGIES: PREPARING LEADERS

And he goeth up into a mountain, and calleth unto him whom he would: and they came unto him. And he ordained twelve, that they should be with him, and that he might send them forth to preach.
--Mark 3:13-14

Leadership is the difference between success and failure in the local church. I believe there are three priorities for successful leaders: we must know why our people should go where we are leading, we must know how to lead them and how to do what we want them to do, and we must know when to lead the people.

In Ezekiel 36, we see God upset with the shepherds (pastors, leaders) of Israel. Many current church leaders are failing to properly lead, and create a great deal of confusion and cut off most church growth. No congregation will ever grow beyond its leaders' capacity to lead. No pastor will ever lead a congregation beyond the level of his own relationship with God.

Ego

Unfortunately, sometimes the biggest obstacle to church growth is the pastor's ego. This is delicate, because any good leader has a healthy ego and enough self-confidence to convince himself that he is the man for the job. The issue isn't self-confidence- it is ego maniacs and cockiness. A well-known evangelist told me that the reason his denomination had so few large churches was because there were so few big men to lead them. Small men build small churches. Big men build growing churches. My father, who was a deacon and a church planter, knew a lot about pastors, and once commented, "If you're too big to preach to a small crowd, you're too small to preach to a big one." A bus captain in a church I pastored in Missouri had nearly 100 people ride his bus one Sunday morning. Everyone was very excited and complimented him, but he just smiled and didn't say anything. The next Sunday morning, only about 25 rode his bus. Someone asked him, "Wow. What went wrong?" He replied, "I didn't take the credit when it was up; I'm not taking the blame when it's down."

Leadership Selection

When selecting a leader, it is important to look for certain characteristics in the prospective leader's life: proof of salvation, technical ability, availability, and commitment. Remember, leaders are not normally born; they are usually made. A pastor must discern who church leaders will be. They must be chosen carefully, because the pastor will have to work with them for a long time. The pastor must bear in mind that his leaders will never grow beyond his capacity to train them. He must obtain the necessary training before he will be enabled to adequately train his lay leaders.

It is helpful to provide a leadership conference on a yearly basis with a theme that is pertinent to the current needs of the congregation. It is important that the pastor set the tone and discerns the needs for the conference, but it is not necessary for him to do all the teaching. In fact, other leaders from the congregation with strengths in certain areas should be enlisted to make different presentations.

I think it is important to provide a "professional" setting for this seminar. So often things that are done for the Lord are done poorly or on the cheap. Because of these tendencies, it is easy to disregard them. They simply don't measure up to the training our members receive in the workplace. I don't like that. I think everything that is done for the Lord should be of the highest caliber. When we put on our annual leadership conference, we organize a catering committee to handle the food, and our people eat very well while they are receiving their training. Everyone who speaks has material prepared for distribution. Like everyone else, we use audio-visual accessories, such as PowerPoint presentations and videos. It becomes obvious that we put a lot of work into our training conference, and, because it is so obvious, people take it more seriously.

Year by year, the church needs will vary, but it is important to begin the first year of the conference program with an orientation to the basic concepts of leadership and church growth. The following lesson can be taught to all the lay leaders of the church.

CHURCH LEADERSHIP LESSON

Welcome! You have been invited to this special meeting for the purpose of familiarizing you with the various aspects of our church.

It is my opinion that each of us needs to know the philosophy and the purpose of the church, as well as the methods necessary to attain our goals. If we all know these things and understand them, it will be much easier for us to go in the same direction and arrive at the same conclusions. In a nutshell, based on the New Testament, it is God's will that a church be involved in two basic things: evangelism and discipleship. Anything that cannot be categorized under one of these two headings is something that the church has no business doing.

History

At this point the pastor should insert a brief history of the church, including both accomplishments and failures. Be sure not to cast any aspersions on any previous pastor or leader. You may be denigrating someone's hero.

Opportunity

Because of our prayers, God has opened a door of opportunity for us, and we must not refuse to enter. If we refuse, He will close the door. We are supposed to discover our place, our purpose, and our progress, if we are to continue to have progress. Listen to what is said in this conference and pray that God will speak through your pastor and to your heart. Let's leave this place with enlightened minds, excited spirits, unified direction and clear purpose.

Definition of the "Church"

According to the New Testament, the church has at least three theological models. The church is the bride of Christ (Ephesians 5), the body of Christ (1 Corinthians 12), and the building of Christ (Ephesians 2, 1 Peter 2?). We will concentrate on the third theological quality: The church is the body of called out believers. It consists of those who have accepted Jesus Christ as Lord and Savior, and who live for Him by faith. The church consists of His disciples. The local church is that group of people who congregate together in worship, service, and fellowship and group together in a common bond of doctrine and purpose.

Differences of Opinion and Loyalty

Christians may not be in 100% agreement on either doctrine or purpose, but they will be close enough in agreement on doctrine, and purpose that disagreements are held to a minimum, and will not deter the church from accomplishing its purpose.

Christians do not all agree completely on biblical interpretation, and it isn't necessary that we do so. However, the lessons taught in our classrooms and the messages delivered in our pulpit must always be in compliance with the doctrine as set forth in our church's statement of faith. For anyone to teach or preach anything else would be a terrible act of treason and misconduct, but no one needs to feel he must agree on everything taught or preached in the church.

It is not necessary that everyone agree on every plan, program, or method employed by the church. As long as human beings are involved, mistakes will happen, so we should just decide to accept that. However, our church has years of experience to guide us, and hours of planning and prayer are put into every plan and program before discussions are made.

Though it is not necessary that you agree with everything in the church, it is not acceptable for you to sabotage the program and methods the church has selected, or the doctrines taught by the pastor and the teaching staff, as long as they are in accordance with the church's doctrinal statement.

We will not all agree on Christian standards in every case. It is, however, the responsibility of the pastor to guide the church into Christian living as a shepherd guides the sheep. It is your duty to be careful of one another's happiness and reputation, and remember that not all have the same degree of light that you have.

If you, as a church leader, find that you disagree with a program, method or decision of the church, you have the privilege of coming directly to the congregationally elected leader of the church, the pastor. You will get a fair hearing. Your concerns will be forwarded to the proper board, committee or personnel. You will receive a report about whatever decision was made or action was taken. All problems are prayerfully considered and handled in a Christ-like manner. We can't resolve all disagreements to everyone's satisfaction, but we try.

We are the church. Our church is a part of the bride, body and building of Christ, and all of us are responsible for what our church does. We must be careful about the church, love it and protect it, but not hinder it.

Definition of a Leader

A church leader is one who has the duty and responsibility of leading, or directing people or programs in the church organization. Every leader has a definite responsibility in this church, either leading people or directing a program. If you accept a responsibility, you are a leader. Some have more responsibility than others.

Any person who makes a profession of faith in Jesus Christ, follows the Lord in baptism, is willingly discipled and presents evidence of living for Christ is eligible for church membership. However, a leader operates under a different standard than non-leaders. A church leader must be above reproach. We expect separation from the world and from worldly practices from those who fill church offices. Leaders have a biblical duty to be faithful to attend church services, to tithe, and to be loyal to other church officers, the pastor and the program.

Response

See yourself as a leader, working within the framework of the church and under the guidance and overall leadership of the pastor. Work with those who are directly over you, and fit into the program. Don't gossip. Don't gripe. Be responsible. Be accountable. Be ready to answer with love and excitement when called on for a report. Be a good leader. Remember the pastor's calling to lead the church (Hebrews 13:17). He is trained to lead the church, and the church is his livelihood. He is even more concerned about the church's success than you are.

Purpose

The purpose of the church is to glorify God. What will glorify God? It seems to me that we should all try to agree on the purpose or priorities of the church and get them in their proper place. The first priority must be soul winning. Second must be evangelistic outreach. Third must be doctrine. And fellowship must be fourth.

1. Soul winning. A church succeeds only as it wins souls, so every leader must become a soul winner. When some of you were saved years ago you were not taught to try to win souls. You didn't have the advantage our new converts have. Before they get embarrassed about Christ, they have already witnessed. What can be done for seasoned believers who were never taught to win souls? First, don't let pride get in the way. Also, don't claim you are afraid to witness if you are really just disinterested in it, lazy, ashamed to talk about Christ, or sinful. If the problem really is fear, find someone who is a soul winner and let them mentor you. If your problem is just laziness, shame, or sin, repent of that and decide to become a biblical Christian.

   All our worship services are intended to either reach, or to prepare to reach souls with the gospel and see them saved. When you are in a worship service, either in a pew or as a leader, do all you can to make that meeting or service a soul-winning venture. Don't do or say anything that will prevent the church, or your ministry, from winning a soul to Christ.

2. Evangelism. We must reach out to other cities and other countries. We pray for missions. We give to missions. We send missionaries. We pray that God will call our young people to the fields of the world. Your pastor and staff are willing to serve on denominational boards and committees. They will conduct revivals or speak at conferences when requested. We work to train workers.

3. Fellowship. The church must offer fellowship to everyone. We offer fellowship through the informal friendly pre-service and post-service times, in family

fellowship, in class and group meetings, through one-on-one fellowship, at sporting events, and by just being friendly with one another. Be sure you aren't guilty of fellowshipping in your own little clique to the exclusion of others. Be friendly with everyone.
4. Doctrine. Doctrine simply means teaching. We teach and preach the Bible as interpreted by our denomination. The doctrine of your church deserves your support. You can show your support by praying for your teacher or preacher, saying "amen," and talking to the speakers after services about sermons or lessons. Let them know that you, and others, are with them.

Philosophy of the Church

The philosophy of our church is simple: "We are here to evangelize and edify." Evangelism requires us to use every method possible, everywhere possible, to win everyone possible to Jesus Christ. We use every department of our church to lead the lost to a saving knowledge of Jesus Christ. Edification requires us to try our very best to build up those who have been reached in the most holy faith and practice. We use the pulpit, Sunday school classes, children's church, follow-up discipleship, and any other appropriate ministry for that purpose. We train and teach our new converts so they can grow to become mature and adept Christian disciples.

Philosophy is important, because it defines who we are. Some see the church as a social club. Others see it as an entertainment center. Some people see it as a place to obtain and maintain power. When we see our church as a place where the power to teach, train, and witness for Christ is obtained, then we have discovered the proper philosophy for the church.

Chapters 7 and 12 could also be included in your leadership training lessons.

STRATEGIES:
BUILDING GOD'S CHURCH

Ye are God's building. According to the grace of God which is given unto me, as a wise master builder, I have laid the foundation, and another buildeth thereon. But let every man take heed how he buildeth thereupon.
--1 Corinthians 3:9b-10

In Matthew 16:18 Christ said, "I will build my church; and the gates of hell shall not prevail against it." The subject before us suggests a spiritual obligation for each of us: building God's church. This church is to be built through God's sovereign grace, through his sanctifying grace, through his stabilizing grace, and through his saving grace.

We are obligated to become better equipped for the work of building God's church. We must become excited about building his church. We need to be doing those things that produce growth in God's church. We must be convinced that it is God's church and not our own.

First Corinthians 1:2 reveals that it is the "church of God." Ephesians 5:23 teaches, "Christ is the head of the church." Verse 24 says the church is subject unto Christ. Verse

25 tells us that Christ loved the church and gave himself for it. In Colossians 1:18 we see that Jesus is the head of the body, the church. Verse 24 says that the church is Christ's body. The church is seen as the bride of Christ, the building of Christ, and the body of Christ.

So, it is His church and He says he will build it, but He uses us to finish what He began. In Acts 1:1, Luke said, "The former treatise have I made, O Theophilus, of all that Jesus began both to do and teach." He will build his church and he will use those he has saved, called, anointed, and empowered to complete the task.

Notice also that it is God's challenge and not ours. "I will build my church, and the gates of hell shall not prevail against it." The devil and all Hell will attack his church, but our Lord readily accepts the challenge. "The gates of hell shall not prevail" (Matthew 16:18). "I will build my church."

Finally, it is God's grace that will do the job if it is done. "For it is not by might, nor by power, but by my spirit, saith the Lord of hosts." (Zechariah 4:6)

The thesis of this chapter is that the pastor should endeavor to build God's Church through His saving, sovereign, sanctifying, and stabilizing grace. Let's look at each significant word in that thesis.

- First, we see the mission: "building." Building requires four ingredients: vision (plans), materials, laborers (workers- we are scriptural referred to as "laborers together"), and work. And we need only turn to Ephesians 4:12 to discover our work in the church. In John 4, Jesus said that the "fields are white unto harvest" (John 4:35). We are told to "look on the fields."
- Second, we see the Master– it is "God's church." We

have already gone into some detail in discussing that it is "his church." We know it, and yet we so often act as though it is ours and not his. Don't treat it like it's your church day after day and then claim it's HIS church when someone challenges your leadership.
- Third, we see the method– "through." How do we build his church? What is the method of building his church? Communism reached over two billion souls in less than 100 years. "Reverend Moon" reached hundreds of thousands of duped people in a little over a decade. But we are reaching so very few. Why?

One of the primary reasons we grow so slowly is a basic, deeply held belief that church growth is an option. Before any denomination, pastor, or church can see any real growth that lasts and endures there must be recognition of a biblical fact. Growth is God's will and non-growth is sin.

The natural expected result of a union of husband and wife is the birth of children. If children aren't ever produced, then there are only three options: they are incapable of bearing children, they are not doing what produces children, or they do not desire children.

It is natural to expect that when Jesus Christ is united with his bride, the church, sons and daughters will be born. Anything else would be contrary to spiritual and biblical nature. We know that our Lord is capable of bearing children. And if the fault lies in the lack of desire on the part of the church, then we indict ourselves. Growth is God's mandate to the church.

Building His church includes evangelism. Evangelism is the all-out effort by the church body, and the clergy, to save the unsaved, to reach the unreached, to find the lost, and to care for the careless. The church must be hyper-evangelistic. The church may teach, train, and fellowship, but will find she is a failure if she does not evangelize. The word "through" implies the method of building God's church. We must attach to the method (through): sovereign grace, sanctifying grace, stabilizing grace, and saving grace. We will discover that each of these methods is required. None can be ignored if the church is to complete its task.

Building God's Church Through His Sovereign Grace

The term "grace" implies a sovereign gift of God. "Grace" provides acceptance (Romans 3:23), enablement (Colossians 1:29), a new position (I Peter 2:5-9), and an inheritance (Ephesians 1:3, 14).

At least three motives are indicated in the New Testament concerning God's Acts of grace, especially in salvation. He does it to express his love. Ephesians 2:4-5 says, "But God, who is rich in mercy, for his great love wherewith he loved us, even when we were dead in sins, hath quickened us together with Christ, by grace ye are saved." He acts in grace to be able to display his grace in the ages to come. Ephesians 2:7 says, "That in the ages to come he might show the exceeding riches of his grace in his kingdom toward us through Christ Jesus." And finally, God acts in grace so that redeemed man will produce good works. In Ephesians 2:10 we read, "For we are his workmanship, created in Christ Jesus unto good works, which God hath ordained that we should walk in them."

Grace is totally unmerited, undeserved, and is a freely given expression of God's love. This grace is God's sovereign property, and he only gives his grace when he chooses to do so. God's grace is never to be wasted. He won't waste it, and it behooves us to be like Him. I once heard a preacher say, "I don't have dying grace now, but when it is my turn to die, God will supply me with dying grace." That's the point. It is God's grace and He gives it to whomever he pleases, when He pleases. He is pleased when His grace will produce salvation for poor lost sinners. He will not give the grace to win souls or build a church to a congregation or pastor who will never use it.

Notice that Jesus said, "I will build my church." There is His sovereign grace. He wills to build His church. Seeing then these previously mentioned motives for God's acts of grace lets us apply these same motives to building His church. Why does God exercise his sovereign grace for the purpose of building his church?

God's grace expresses His love for the Church. It shows a union between Christ and his church. A marriage relationship has occurred. It brings souls into the family of God. A love relationship– a unity of Christ and his church– will always produce souls into the family of God. The world will see God loving his church. Even the world often recognizes that a growing, thriving, soul winning church is the result of God's loving relationship with His church. God expresses his sovereign grace.

God's grace expresses His love in the ages to come. I love to read about God blessing his children in ages past. In Acts 1:46-47 Luke tells us about the church in Jerusalem, "And they continuing daily with one accord in the temple, and breaking bread from house to house did eat their meat with gladness and singleness of heart, praising God, and having favor with all the people. And the Lord added to the church daily such as should be saved." Acts 3:4 tells of 5,000 men being saved, and in chapter 4:31-33 we read, "And when they had prayed,

the place was shaken where they were assembled together, and they were all filled with the Holy Ghost, and they spoke the word of God with boldness. And the multitudes of them that believed were of one heart and of one soul. Neither said any of them that aught of the things which he possessed was his own, but they had all things common. And with great power gave the apostles witness of the resurrection of the Lord Jesus, and great grace was upon them all."

I love to read about the great churches of the past such as Moody's church in Chicago, the Brooklyn Tabernacle where Talmadge preached, and the great church in London where Spurgeon ministered. I love to read about Randall, Whitefield, and Wesley. The problem is that those victories are all in the past. Do you realize that your church could be one that preachers talk about in ages to come? Not only that, but in eternity the saints of God will rejoice at what God did through our church, the numbers saved, the souls baptized, the confessions given, and the growth experienced. All of that will express his grace to the church.

God exercises his sovereign grace in building his church so that redeemed man will produce good works. It is the Lord's plan that His church produces good works. It was our Lord who said, "Let your light so shine before men, that they may see your good works, and glorify your father which is in heaven" (Matthew 5:16). Good works are the evidence of faith and the product of the grace of God. They bring glory to God rather than man. The good works of the church are obvious: saved souls, spiritual maturity, evangelistic fervency, church unity, and dedicated stewardship. All these add up to church growth— growth in numbers, in maturity, and in spirituality. Our Lord exercises his sovereign grace so that redeemed men will produce good works. When we put all this together we are able to see that God builds His church through his sovereign grace. In the New Testament church great growth was the norm, not the unusual.

The Lord blesses the man of God and the church of God that loves him, obeys him, and is anxious to follow his leadership. As one becomes more devoted to the Lord, as love for him increases, as growth methods are learned, and as these methods are carried out, God, through his sovereign grace, produces growth in the church. God always furnishes whatever is needed to build his church. Pastors are discouraged and churches are depressed, because pastors and churches cannot experience revival and growth until they get a holy excitement from the Lord. This excitement is produced by the great grace of God. It is God's sovereign grace and He extends it as He wills. Anyone who uses that grace to build God's church will receive God's sovereign grace to do so.

Building God's Church Through His Sanctifying Grace.

He provides grace and His grace is sufficient. To be sanctified is to be consecrated, to be purified, and to be separated. Sanctification is a progressive process that changes the life of the regenerated sinner, moment by moment. In sanctification there occurs a substantial healing of the separation that has occurred between God and man, between man and his fellow man, between man and himself, and between man and nature.

There are three aspects of the sanctifying work of Christ and his spirit: positional (I Corinthians 1:2); experimental (Romans 6:2-10); and ultimate (1 John 3:1-10). In the same way the Lord sanctifies the believer He also sanctifies the church. He progressively sanctifies the church. The church of Jesus Christ should gradually become more sanctified every day. The church undergoes experiential sanctification and will undergo ultimate sanctification.

In the book of Acts four events stand out prominently: the Lord went up, the Holy Spirit came down, the Christians went out, and the sinners came in. I want to emphasize the second point–the Spirit came down. This is repeatedly referred to as the gift of the Holy Spirit. The church is sanctified by grace. This grace is totally unmerited, undeserved, and freely given. God sanctifies his church, and in the process God provides the missing ingredients for growth the church needs.

- **First, God provides purity through his sanctifying grace.** The Lord uses pure vessels. He uses pure men and women of God. He uses pure churches. In Leviticus 8:15, Moses "purified the altar and sanctified it, to make reconciliation upon it." In Numbers 8:21 "the Levites were purified, and they washed their clothes: and Aaron offered them as an offering before the Lord; and Aaron made atonement for them to cleanse them." In Ezra 6:20, the "priests were purified." In John 11:55, the Jews went up to Jerusalem to purify themselves before Passover. And in Titus 2:14, Paul said concerning Christ "who gave himself for us, that he might redeem us from all iniquity, and purify unto himself a peculiar people zealous of good works."

The ultimate result of this purifying grace is good works. Lacking this grace means that no good works are produced. The Scripture points out at least four ways God's church is purified:

Through truth and love- 1 Peter 1:22, "Seeing ye have purified your soul in obeying the truth through the spirit unto unfeigned love of the brethren."

Through faith- in Acts 15:9 Peter preached concerning the Gentiles that God "purified their hearts by faith."

Through proximity to God- James 4:8 we read, "Draw nigh to God and he will draw nigh to you. Cleanse your hands, ye sinners, and purify your hearts, ye double minded."

Through walking in Christ's light- 1 John 1:7, "But if we walk in the light as he is in the light, we have fellowship one with another, and the blood of Jesus Christ his son cleanseth us from all sin."

The pure church will attract honest folk who want to be freed from the burden of their sins. The pure church will show the difference between the true church of God and the apostate church. God provides purity for his church through his sanctifying grace.

- **Second, God provides passion through his sanctifying grace.** Real passion is a rare ingredient in the average church. We lack passion for God, for other Christians, for the lost. One of the main reasons for the lack of passion in the church is provably our lack of purity. Too many of us just simply don't care. We would like to have a large congregation, a beautiful church, and a large church income, but the idea of souls going to hell really doesn't bother us. We have our special friends, our pastor buddies who agree with us–at least to our face- but we would utterly destroy another preacher brother, or a brother in Christ, if they stumble. If a prostitute or a drunken derelict walked down the aisle and gave their heart to Christ, we would all welcome them into the body. We would shout praise to God and go home rejoicing. But if one of our brothers or sisters in Christ were to fall into sin, many of us would put our heel on their neck and help drive them deeper into despair. We often ignore commands to "bear one another's burdens" (Galatians 6:2), "endeavor to keep the unity of the spirit in the bond of peace" (Ephesians 4:2), and follow the basic Christian admonitions to "be careful of one another's reputation," and "seek to strengthen the weak, encourage the afflicted, and admonish the erring." My friend, you are your brother's keeper, like it or not.

We lack passion for God. Our hearts don't burn with love and devotion. We are not consumed with loyal dedication to God and his church, which is obvious from the pastoral changes we make– quitting the ministry to sell insurance or real estate or to teach school. Passion is an overpowering devotion, an intense affection or longing. Such is to be our attitude toward God and His church. God places passion within our heart for Himself, for the church he made us the shepherd over, for other Christians, and definitely for lost souls. This passion will keep us going when everyone else is discouraged and depressed. This passion will keep us loving when others are filled with hate. God provides this passion through His sanctifying grace.

- **Third, God provides power through his sanctifying grace.** It is needless to try to build

God's church without the manifestation of His power in our lives and in our congregation. When we read the book of Acts, it is easy to identify the power of God manifesting itself in the church. Jesus went up, the spirit came down, and the accompanying powers so infilled them, anointed them, and overwhelmed them, that they immediately began seeing results. They saw amazement on the faces of unbelievers who could not understand the miraculous working of God. They saw conviction fall on unbelievers as they were "pricked in their heart," and at the preaching of Peter and the brethren, and sinners said, "Men and brethren, what shall we do?" (Acts 2:37). They saw salvation come upon thousands, and this salvation provided obedience "and they that gladly received his word were baptized: and the same day there were added unto them about two thousand souls" (Acts 2:41). They saw fear and awe fall upon the church as well as upon the unbelievers. God's power fell.

God's power also revealed itself when the church began to take on the image of Jesus. "Now when they saw the boldness of Peter and John, and perceived that they were unlearned and ignorant men, they marveled; and they took knowledge of them that they had been with Jesus" (Acts 4:13).

In Acts 8:5-25 we learn about the great revival that occurred in Samaria. Verse 8 tells us "there was great joy in the city." Why? Revival had come. We have joyless churches. The charismatic churches have taken advantage of our coldness, our unfriendly atmosphere, our dead formality, and our lifeless services. There must be joy in serving the Lord, and if we are truly serving the Lord, there will be joy. Wherever Jesus is, there is joy. Whenever joy is present, we may be assured that Jesus is also about.

So let's review some of the characteristics of the church that is the recipient of God's power. There will be joy, peace, spiritual service, boldness, Christlikeness, souls saved, great crowds, baptism, new members, financial resources, harmony and unity. Our churches can have all of this. God's power is sufficient to provide it. However, the church, the pastor, and all the members must want it. They must pray for it. There must be prayers like those reported in Acts 4:2-33. We can build God's church through his sanctifying grace. Grace in God provides purity, passion and power for the church.

Building God's Church Through His Stabilizing Grace.
In Matthew 16:18, Jesus said, "And I say unto thee, that thou art Peter, and upon this rock, I will build my church; and the gates of hell shall not prevail against it." This means that the church that is built on faith in Christ will be stable.

The word stable means firmness, steadiness of character, resolution, purpose, freedom from feebleness or changeableness, constancy and resolve. The key word here is character, which means the "peculiar qualities impressed by nature, or by habit, on a person, which distinguishes him from others; hence a character is not formed when the person has not acquired stable and distinctive qualities."

The character of a child is formed in infancy and childhood. As a result, it is easier for some young people, married or single, to acquire a fixed attitude toward Christ, His church, and their faithfulness to him. If a child was taught properly, and acquired a good stable character as a child, even though he is not a Christian, he will probably still be one who pays his bills, keeps his home clean, is faithful on the job, and etc. So when he gets saved, it will be easier to get him to pay tithes, attend regularly and have a sense of responsibility, than the one who was not taught these things as a child, and who did not develop these characteristics of cleanliness, honesty, hard work, faithfulness, and obedience. There are exceptions, but this is the rule.

Several months ago I was having major memory problems. Alzheimer's disease was the frightening word. Every doctor seemed intent on hanging that on me as a diagnosis. I had to undergo many tests and saw a neurologist, psychologist, and psychiatrist. (The last doctor I consulted, a psychiatrist, told me to stop worrying, and get on with my life.) Spending time around these types of doctors means you will hear a lot about behavior and attitude. I learned that these are among the important developmental steps from less mature to more mature conduct

- A shift from morals based on specific rules to more general conception of what is right and wrong.
- A shift from moral conduct that is primarily a response to external demands toward a moral code that is based on internal standards that the child has adopted as his own.
- An increased ability to perceive rules of the game as rules based on mutual respect and mutual consent, rather than on arbitrary edicts.
- An increased ability and willingness to judge the actions of others, to take account of the circumstances in which these actions occur, and

of the motives and intentions underlying them, instead of judging them according to inflexible standards.

For years churches have reached the unreached and then lost them through a combination of neglect and poor teaching. When a person gets saved, the spiritual parent, the church, should be every bit as concerned about preserving and building Christian character as she was in getting that person reborn. The four processes named above apply particularly to the church's discipleship mission.

The task of soul winning is tremendous, too tremendous to attempt under our own power. "It is not by might, nor by power, but by my spirit saith the Lord" (Zechariah 4:6). It is an insurmountable task, if we attempt it alone. We need all kinds of evangelism: one-on-one soul winning, friendship, programmic and mass evangelism, and I trust we utilize all these methods. But it is so foolish to win the lost and leave their spiritual growth to mere chance.

I once counseled an older couple, members of another Baptist church, who had many problems with one of their sons. The woman referred to her son-in-law and said, "He is worthless. He is lazy. He is immoral. He lies. He is a thief. He is just no good. There is no hope for him." Then she paused, thought a moment, and continued: "But his brother was worse than him, and look how he has turned out." I know his brother and he is one of the most conscientious, dedicated, loyal Christian men I know. He is a good provider, a real witness, and faithful to his church. Of course, the difference is Jesus Christ. But also, we were faithful to teach him, and now he is teaching others also. In fact, all the people who teach our follow-up lessons are people who have been taught follow-up.

It isn't just a method with them- it's a shared experience.

In 2 Timothy 2:1-5 the apostle Paul said some very important things that apply to this subject of building God's church through his stabilizing grace. In verse 1 he said it is expected that a new Christian grow to become strong in the grace of our Lord. In verse 2 he said the pastor was to commit the word of God to his converts and they, in turn, were to teach others. This fulfills the great commission. In verse 3 he said the Christian servant is to endure hardness as a good soldier. In verse 4 he said a good soldier never gets entangled in the affairs of the enemy, but seeks to be separate so he can please the one who called him. In verse 5 he said we must strive within the framework of the rules in order to receive the crown. In verse 6 he said those who serve in leadership positions must be one who has partaken of the fruit. We are living in the 21st century, and we minister to a population that is intelligent, educated, sophisticated and alert. Our task is to reach people with the gospel and win them to Christ. That's the evangelistic part of the philosophy of the church. There is another part to this philosophy—we must edify those we reach.

In the congregation I pastor now, we use a one-on-one follow-up method. We teach every new convert person-to-person the assurance of salvation, the methods of Christian growth, denominational distinctive, evangelism, child rearing, stewardship, and successful marriage principles. As a result of this program we have decreased the number of those we lose. After the follow-up director finishes with the 10-week follow-up, the converts are sent to the pastor for a 6-week character-building course that addresses commitment, depression, anger, fear, worry, and Christian love and marriage. We are trying to leave no stone unturned in an effort to build up every new saint in the most holy faith. In my book, Points for Pastors and

Their People, an entire chapter is dedicated to this subject.

I believe there are four vital needs that a successful follow-up program will meet:

- We will help new Christians grow from merely living under the letter of the law to an acceptance of the Christ taught message of the spirit of the law. For example, hating and cursing an enemy is sin, but the attitude of the believer toward that person is even more important. We were taught by our Lord to love our enemies. He said, "Pray for those who despitefully use you" (Matthew 5:44). Paul said, "Recompense to no man evil for evil; provide things honest in the sight of all men. If it be possible, as much as lieth in you, live peaceable with all men. If thine enemy hungers or thirsts, give to him" (Romans 12:18-20). Jesus said that not only must the Christian not commit adultery, but "he that looketh on a woman to lust after her, hath committed adultery already with her in his heart" (Matthew 5:28). We see many of our Christians living by the letter of the law while disregarding the spirit of the law. The mature Christian will recognize that the spirit of the law is stronger and stricter, and will be the basis of judgment. It isn't enough not to lie, we must not backbite or gossip either. We preachers could learn some lessons about attitudes toward other preachers. We are setting poor examples for our flock
- We attempt to shift the Christian from obeying because the church or preacher says so, to a

sense of obligation to obey because God says it, and that makes it right. Pastor Paul Thompson of Phoenix, AZ, says, "If God said it, that settles it, and you'd better obey it." The Christian can't do things simply to impress others, or to be able to stay in the group, but rather he must mature to a sense of trying to please God. The Christian must progress to the point that he does, thinks, and says only what will bring glory to the Lord. For example, the people who tithe because the church needs the money may quit tithing, or begin complaining about how the money is spent. On the other hand, the person who tithes because God so commands, and desires to glorify and please God, will give whether the church needs the money or not. That's how programs, missions and colleges are supported.

- We will strive to help the new Christian mature beyond obeying the laws of God from guilt or fear, to obedience out of concern for the influence of Christ and his church. Every Christian should ask himself what his sinful indulgence will do to a weaker Christian or to an unsaved person or how it will affect the influence of Christ in society. If fear motivates us to obedience, or if we serve only out of guilt, sooner or later we will probably give up. The Christian must become a part of the total program of Christ's church. He must see himself as a steward, as one who is a goodwill ambassador for the Lord. He must see himself

as his brother's keeper.
- We will strive to help the convert grow to an ability to accept the weaknesses of others without feeling like he is approving of them. This is a real sign of maturity. The ability to accept another Christian with all the differences we have, without feeling like I am compromising, or even approving of his beliefs, is a sign of spiritual maturity.

I won't elaborate any more on these. The difference between a church that mushrooms and then dies, whether a quick or lingering death, and one that continues to experience growth year after year, is a simple matter of spiritual maturity on the part of the church and its leadership. Maturity requires more than reading the Bible through every year. It is more that praying every day. It is more than seeing liquor as a damning sin. It is more than condemning divorce. Maturity is all these things I have mentioned, and much more. It is probable that no one reaches this maturity alone. This maturity is a result of three vital programs all working together: the grace of our Lord (2 Corinthians 12:7-10, especially verse nine); the guidance of the church (2 Timothy 2:20); and the dedication of the believer (Ephesians 5:13-21).

The stabilizing grace of our Lord will mature the new Christian, and they will work with him and you in building his church. If the church is built like this it will endure and the gates of hell will not prevail against it.

Building God's Church Through His Saving Grace

Jesus came to seek and to save. "Saving" suggests a need– a desperate and demanding need. Everyone needs to be- in fact, must be- saved. Saved–or perish. Saved–or ruined. Saved–

or lost in hell. The church and clergy will never see the desperation behind the words of our Lord in Luke 19:10 when he aid, "For the son of man is come to seek and to save that which was lost," until she sees that saving men is the only hope for their eternity; saving men is the first work of Jesus; saving men is the first and greatest work of the church. By reading most Sunday bulletins you would think that teaching about eschatology or teaching about the Holy Spirit or the deeper life is the first and great work of the church. You would think that ball games, fishing, and bowling were the first and great work of the church. You would think that fellowship, ordinances, and doctrines were the first and great work of the church. In fact, sometimes you would think fussing, fighting, and feuding, were the first great works of the church. No matter how important any or all of these things are, the first and great work of the church is seeking and saving those that are lost. And as John said in 1 John 5:19, "the whole world lieth in wickedness." So the "means" that is first and makes the room for all the rest is soul winning. Evangelism must occur first before any of these other methods can be utilized.

Saving. That word passes into nothingness without the accompanying word and work of grace. We know, of course, that grace is all the work of God. It is totally unmerited. It is undeserved and unearned. This grace is bestowed on the sinner in at least three ways: by Christ's death on the cross and all that incurs; by the searching, convicting, and converting ministry of God; and by the filling and keeping ministry of God. Hours could be spent on the subject of God's saving grace as it is imparted to the sinner, but we must see God's saving grace as a necessary ally with us in building his church.

Three areas are obvious when we consider the grace of

God bestowed to assist us in our efforts to labor with and for him in building his church:

His Holy Pattern.

If you want to see the pattern our Lord gave, look at John 4 and the perfect pattern for leading a person to salvation. He had a divine compulsion– "Needs to go through Samaria." He had a direct challenge– "Call thy husband and come hither." He had a distinct confession–"I am he." And, he had a definite conclusion–"Is not this the Christ?"

His Holy Power.

In Acts 4:33 we read, "With great powers gave the apostle's witness of the resurrection of the Lord Jesus." The apostles were recipients of the power of Christ. The Lord manifested this power at the tomb of Lazarus when he raised him from the dead, and again, when he was transfigured before them. This holy power of our Lord is available for the church today.

We need it. We must have it. If we are going to have full churches, if we are going to have full altars, if we are going to have busy baptisteries, then we must have his holy power. When you attend a growing evangelistic church, you can sense the power of God. It is more than friendliness. It is more than organization. It is more than large crowds. It is the holy power of God and it originates with a craving, a yearning, a hungering and thirsting for that power. That power manifests itself in spirit filled services, full altars, and changed lives. That power comes from Early Bird Prayer Meeting each Sunday morning at 8:45. It comes from the deacon and pastor prayer meeting between Sunday school and worship. It comes from the Wednesday night prayer service. This holy power comes as a result of a hungry church praying for God's holy power. And, manifestation of that power is clearly seen in saved souls, large crowds, and a thriving, growing church.

His Holy Provision

The Lord has seen to it that all we need to have to build his church is provided. As Phil 4:19 says, "My God shall supply all your needs according to his riches in glory by Christ Jesus." He has provided the vision. He says, "Look on the fields, they are white unto harvest" (John 4:35). Well, that's obvious- sin is abounding, ungodliness is rampant, and wickedness is everywhere. The miracle is that we can see it, and we can see it as Christ wills us to see it. The darkness of the hour makes the light shine all the brighter. So we can see the hour as Christ wants us to see it. He has provided the tools. We have such tools as Sunday school literature, the bus ministry, children's church, teen ministries, senior citizens' programs, soul-winning conferences, enlightened laymen, exciting preaching, counseling, books, and video and audio tapes. The tools are there.

He has provided his own blood to wash away the sins of the sinner. He has provided his presence to encourage the church in her task of building his kingdom. Therefore, we have the supreme task before us: building (the mission) God's church (the master) through (the method) His saving grace (the means). But there is one last great matter that becomes increasingly necessary, as we grow older.

The Holy Purpose

I conclude with this brief observation: seeing the mission, the master, the method, and the means will avail nothing unless there is a divine motive. I need a purpose for what I am doing.

I am weary. I am tired of building programs. I am tired of the pressure of raising budgets, and starting and carrying out programs. I am tired of the endless counseling. I am tired of chasing after people who seem intent on going to hell, in spite of all we can do. I am tired of hearing about the quarrels in my denomination. I guess I am getting old and over the hill. I need a purpose. I need a fresh new motivation. I stagger to the Word of God and He gives this tired weary laborer a new purpose, a fresh new look at the nail-scarred hand of Jesus. If you need a fight to keep you excited, then your purpose is all wrong. Take a look at Jesus and His word. Pastor, deacon– listen to what it is all about. Building God's church, that's your program. That's your mission. That's your reason. God calls you to build his church. And the whole process, the whole task, begins with saving souls through his saving grace. I can build my church any way I want to. I can't build His church without eva

STRATEGY:
OPENING THE ALTARS OF THE CHURCH

Now when they heard this, they were pricked in their heart, and said unto Peter and to the rest of the apostles, Men and brethren, what shall we do?

Then Peter said unto them, Repent and be baptized every one of you in the name of Jesus Christ for the remission of sins, and ye shall receive the gift of the Holy Ghost.

For the promise is unto you, and your children, and to all that are afar off, even as many as the Lord our God shall call.

And with many other words did he testify and exhort, saying,

Save yourselves from this untoward generation.

Then they that gladly received his word were baptized: and the same day there were added unto them about three thousand souls.

And they continued steadfastly in the apostles' doctrine and fellowship and in breaking of bread, and in prayers.

--Acts 2:37-42

The pastor who wishes to build or revive an evangelical church in a reasonable length of time with no money, no help and no outside support will find it necessary to create a spiritual atmosphere in the church. The most visible evidence of a heightened spiritual atmosphere is an increased frequency of visits to the altar by members of the church seeking God's direction and by the lost seeking salvation. Churches should set out to grow through conversion, not transfers by disgusted believers from other assemblies. There is no excitement in a dead church to attract transfer growth, anyway.

Therefore, the altars must be "open for business." In the days of the Tabernacle, during the time of tribal justice, a fugitive could run into the sanctuary and grab the horns of the altar and be considered to be untouchable. The Cities of Refuge served the same purpose. The altars provided a very present help in time of trouble. Scripture presents the altar as symbols of refuge, prayer, and sacrifice to God. They made a difference.

Altars are little more than ornaments in many Protestant churches these days, just something we have to move out of the way whenever a wedding is held in our auditoriums. They are considered unsophisticated, symbolic of a bygone era when our people didn't make as much money as they do now and hadn't been to school. We are much more comfortable recommending therapists or counselors to seekers than enabling them to pray over their problems in a safe context of concerned and loving believers.

Back in the early 1960's a pastor friend of mine in St. Louis, Missouri, Harry Asher, led his congregation in a building program. As was common in those days, the members volunteered most of the work on the building. Even most of the furniture was either assembled or completely built by the congregation. The furniture in this building was made from light pine. The congregation was very anxious to move in, and began holding services in the new sanctuary before it was entirely finished. The altar had not yet been varnished when a particular service saw a number of individuals give their hearts to Christ. When the service ended, some of the ladies of the congregation were horrified to see tear stains on the unfinished pine of the altar. They wanted to make sure it was sanded off before it was varnished. Harry came in the next day with a can of clear varnish and covered the altar with it, preserving the tearstains forever. He said that that was what he always wanted people to see in his church- tear-stained altars.

A Matter of Perspective

Churches are built through evangelizing the lost and restoring the backslider. But how does the rank and file know how these "newcomers" are becoming part of the congregation? It is important that they see the seekers make public professions of faith by going to the altar. In order to do this, going to the altar needs to become something that is not unusual. The altar must become "de-stigmatized." It is unlikely that the unsaved are going to perform this service for the congregation; the congregation must do it for the unsaved. That means that Christians- in particular, church leaders- must become dependent upon and frequently seen at the altar.

This is the really vital concept in this chapter. God's people must set the altar up in a special place in their hearts. They must know what it is for. They cannot be surprised when anyone goes to the altar. The pastor must be willing to bow there before the congregation. Deacons and elders and teachers must frequent the altar if their spiritual leadership is to be seen as a service to God's people rather than as a position of prominence. The altar is the great physical equalizer of the congregation. E. M. Bounds wrote that a man is no taller than he is on his knees, and that is even truer of an individual congregation.

A Matter of Preaching

Preaching plays a lead role in opening the altars- the kind of preaching that is more than teaching. Preaching must always inform, but altar-opening preaching must be far above the common lecture.

Altar-opening preaching must be exhortative. It must provoke conviction, awake to responsibility, proclaim God's holiness, expose humanity's sinfulness, and realize both heaven and hell. Obviously, this preaching is totally wrapped around faith issues, and not just those of the congregation. This is where the pastor must do the leading that only the pastor can do, because he is the one called to this particular pulpit at this particular time for these particular people.

Rationalizations that "it does little good to preach to the converted" are foolishness. A careful review of Scripture will find few sermons in Scripture (Jonah and some in Acts as notable exceptions) that were not addressed to professing believers, whether Hebrew or Christian. The converted need to go to the altar frequently- especially if they are right with God.

Altar-opening preaching must prompt decision-making. Joshua's exhortation to "choose this day who you will serve" (Joshua 24:15) was addressed, we recall, to believers. So must the pastoral preaching which opens altars. If people are not pressed to make a decision based on what they have heard, then the preacher has done no more than the evening newscaster. He has told people how bad it is, and then they can go back to being entertained by the shows they really like to watch. To prompt decisions, this preaching must be:

- Clear. This is not the time for ambiguity or cleverness, but for frankness and direction.
- Timely. Decisions are to be occasional; that is, they are based on the situation the hearer is facing at the moment of the sermon, whether family pressures, financial distress, sinful habits, wandering hearts, impending death or life-altering choices are the subject at hand. Altar-opening preaching teaches that the altar is the place to go for any and all spiritual, emotional or personal needs.
- Convenient. This is not to say that having open altars is to be frivolous in any way. Rather, it means that the road to the altar must be free of hindrances, whether that involves making sure small children are not allowed to disturb the service, removing physical impediments to getting to the altar (such as taking out the front two pews, if necessary), or simply making sure that the congregation is trained to close its eyes prayerfully during times of altar call. The directions concerning coming to the altar to make a decision or confession must be very clear, and the pastor must practice doing this to do it well. Church members should think enough of the altar to know to get out of the way when someone is trying to get past them during the altar service, and should be sensitive enough to the flow of the service to notice who is under conviction.

- Necessary. People must understand that making a public profession, responding to God's call and direction, are a requirement.

Altar-opening preaching must also be doctrinal. If we are conscientious about the nature of our altar calls, then we will be theologically faithful. This is important, because many people have an inordinate (or possibly legitimate) fear that altar calls are manipulative. If we focus on the fact that Christ's method for gaining disciples was a simple invitation, and if we understand that the keys of faith in Christ and trust in His Word are to be paramount in our approaches, then we will not be willing to manipulate. Sad stories are not necessary when the love of Christ and His sacrifice have been clearly revealed. And, by the way, it is not manipulative to direct people to do what must be done to save their lives. Driving instructors do it. Surgeons do it. Lifeguards do it. We are helping people understand the way into the Kingdom of God, something that is unnatural, yet vital to every human being. Charges of manipulation will usually be avoided by simply being true to the Word, and those that cannot be avoided should be given the attention they are worth: none.

Altar-opening preaching must offer the altar to everyone within hearing of the sermon. The altars are to be physically accessible, as we mentioned above, but they also must be user-friendly. Going to the altar has to be explained. For years, Billy Graham has conducted his evangelistic invitations by saying, "I'm going to ask you to get out of your seat, come forward to the platform, and someone will show you how to receive Christ." This method is simple, direct, informative, honest, and effective. To offer the altar to everyone, to truly make it user-friendly, the following should be done:

Preach about coming to the altar and why people should come to the altar repetitively. The church, at least, must understand the doctrine of the altar. The attitude of the church has toward the altar determines the attitude of the seeker.

Invite and urge the church to come to the altar often. Every service in which Christians gather is a good opportunity to utilize the altar. Regularly scheduled prayer services are obviously appropriate times, but it is also important that the church come together in prayer at special times, following particularly emotional services, when someone is in great spiritual, physical or emotional need, for renewing wedding vows, commitment of children, before evangelistic campaigns, and other occasions. There really is no wrong time to use the altar to bring people together spiritually. People must believe that going to the altar is a privilege and a right for believers.

Never discourage anyone from coming to the altar, even if they come over and over. The more people come, the friendlier it will seem. Of course some people will come to the altar to get attention. The Old and New Testaments have examples of those who claimed spirituality for personal reasons (Balaam, Simon the Sorcerer, Ananias and Sapphira). God dealt with them individually; neither prophecy nor generosity was discouraged because someone abused their practice. The tendency to try to eliminate the possibility of abuse is reflective of the "reformer" attitude in American politics. It is not Biblical. Reformers try to eliminate the possibility for sin. Biblicists accept sin as both a reality and a probability, and prescribe Biblical solutions- repentance and confession.

Profession is to be public. That was the entire point of baptism in the New Testament. It was a sign, especially when performed by an ethnic Jew, that a conversion of the heart had taken place. It was a funeral for the old life, a ceremony open to observers. Going to the altar is part and parcel of the same concept. I think it is a mistake to dismiss someone to a counseling room when he or she responds to an invitation. The congregation has no joy to share when people are excused to a decision room. The convert is born in a sterile (that is, deadening) environment when he or she is removed from the fellowship of believers at the moment of new birth. Bear in mind that, humans being what they are, will rationalize that if a conversion can be restricted to a private matter, then the Christian life as a whole can be confined to privacy as well. This is how we think, how we link concepts.

Always give an invitation to come to the altar whenever the church is together in worship. This means that the pastor must learn how to give an invitation. Here is the real reason many pastors don't think invitations are a valid method- they simply don't know how to give one. We all like to do the things we're good at. Pastors who don't like to do altar calls (or don't do them) most likely don't feel like they are good at them, because they don't know how to do one. They may justify themselves by reasoning that altar calls are manipulative, or that to be really good at them a preacher must be flamboyant or tell sad stories to make people cry and have an emotional response. Nothing could be further from the truth. First of all, an altar call is a call to respond to the truth the person has just heard from God's Word. Truth is not manipulative. Second, an altar call is a call to make a life-changing decision that will improve the hearer's life. It's not a sales technique; it's a decision similar to deciding whether or not to have a tumor removed. People's lives really are at stake, and part of the problem is that many pastors and church members just don't believe that anymore.

A Matter of Proficiency

Anything that is done well is practiced. To learn how to give an invitation is a sign of integrity and submission to the Holy Spirit and respect for the experience of others. As mentioned above, most pastors don't know how to give an invitation, so they either do it poorly or don't do it at all. It is important to find an example or, at least, some direction when learning how to give an invitation. For a local pastor to emulate Billy Graham is probably not a good idea, but Graham certainly legitimizes invitations to the general public, since he has been doing them for his entire ministry and has a reputation and an organizational structure that is conducive to giving invitations.

If there is no one you can watch, then you should find a few simple, legitimate policies and procedures to follow. Once you get used to these, you will probably think of ways to improve upon them, but never forget the basics.

View the invitation as the climax of the sermon. The final point of the sermon should slide seamlessly into the altar call. The invitation is the target for which the pastor is shooting. Decisions are the point, not for a tally-board, but for spiritual welfare. People should always be challenged to make a decision, either for or against Christ, when they hear the Gospel. This is unnatural for many pastors, so it must be practiced and planned. It is probably a good idea for a pastor to preach through his sermons by himself in an empty sanctuary the night before they are to be delivered. He can made additions, edit out unnecessary items, and visualize the people in the congregation for whom the message is prepared and pray for them. He can practice transitions from point to point until it is unnecessary for him to be bound to his notes. He can move naturally and spiritually.

Again, anything that is done well is practiced.

Close the message with prayer. Don't preach another sermon in the prayer. Pray about the message you have just delivered, how people need to respond, and why. Ask God to drive the message home, to give seekers courage to respond, to give Christians the integrity to respond, to give the congregation the courtesy to not hinder anyone who needs to respond. If God has touched you while you were preaching, respond to that. Ask God to cleanse you so you will be fit to guide seekers to the altar and into His Kingdom.

After the prayer, explain what the seeker must do. Explain where to come (if they are visitors, they may never have noticed the altars, and don't know what you are talking about), what to do (bow at the altar), and who will help them (altar workers must be ready- see below). Also, tell them what they will be expected to do once they arrive at the altar.

The invitation should include a time of private examination and prayer. Paul's admonition in 1 Corinthians 11 to "examine ourselves" is good advice every time we worship, not just when we come around the Lord's Table. People often will not consider their spiritual condition unless they are specifically directed to and instructed how. Supply those instructions to the congregation with their heads bowed and their eyes closed.

Be sure your altar workers are trained to receive those who come to the altar. The pastor cannot do the altar work, because he has to complete his sermon in the invitation. Therefore, he must have trained workers who are dependable and understand what the point of the sermon is. At the very least, these altar workers must:

- Be in prayer throughout the entire service for the expected harvest at the conclusion.
- Be ready when the invitation begins, with their Bibles marked and ready in their hands.
- Be thoroughly trained with a plan for salvation, a plan for backslider recommitment, some verses for simple spiritual counseling, and an understanding of the need and procedure for making immediate referrals.
- Be conscious of breath and body odor.
- Be conscious of the invitation activities. Their eyes should be open during the prayers, unless the pastor specifically directs them to close their eyes. They have to be conscious of the direction of the altar worker director.
- Be organized. An altar worker must be trained and ready. He must be someone who manages the altar. He or she makes sure tissue, Bibles, decision cards and pencils are available at the altar. If your church auditorium is large, you may find it necessary to have an altar worker (and backup) on both sides of the building during the invitation.
- Be submissive. The altar worker director chooses who prays with seekers. The rule of thumb is: gender-specific. Males do not pray with females and vice versa. If a person needs special counseling from a member of the opposite sex, the altar worker who made the referral should stay with them as chaperone.

Make sure the music is appropriate. A soloist is preferable to a congregational song, because announcing a hymn number and the ensuing fumbling through hymnals is distracting to the minds of those under conviction. If you prefer that the congregation sing together, either stick to a few familiar songs that are well known without the use of hymnals, or use a PowerPoint so the congregation can look straight ahead and keep their hands and attention free. The choice of songs is very important. "Just As I Am" is, of course, the classic, but it is refreshing that so many contemporary Christian songs emphasize making decisions. "He Is Able" is a wonderful chorus for invitations after sermons that emphasize commitment and faith in God. The chorus "White As Snow," combined with "Nothing But the Blood" is a beautiful and meaningful medley for salvation sermons.

It is important that the pastor play a role in the selection of the songs that will be played at the most important moments of the preaching service. Don't hesitate to make your wishes known to the music director. Pick them out well in advance, and make sure the musicians and soloist or music director know them well.

It's also important to have more than one song ready, because invitations that are prolonged (because of seeker response) can become monotonous with one song played over and over. Also, if an invitation reaps a great harvest for the Lord, it is a good idea to move from a song of invitation to a song of victory (at the pastor's direction). A song of victory must be ready if this is to be effective.

Take plenty of time. Don't rush. An invitation with movement could take half as long as the sermon. Plan for that. Get more said in your sermons in less time. Practice before you preach. Many sermons are long because of lack of preparation, not because the preacher is filled with so many profundities. Our culture has been trained by television shows to sit still for about eight minutes. It's going to take a pretty interesting sermon to hold their attention, and having a long invitation had better be necessary. Nothing is more pathetic than a preacher begging people to come to the altar when the sermon hasn't given them a real reason to come.

It will take a long time to train your congregation to understand the importance of the invitation, just like it takes a long time to get them comfortable with a sermon longer than 15 minutes. But a pastor who sees time as his best friend will eventually be successful. A successful restaurateur once explained how to market gourmet food to a fast-food population: "You give them what they want, and you teach them. And you give them what they want, and you teach them. And you give them what they want, and you teach them. And then, one day, you give them what you want." This is incrementalism. It is leadership. It is discipleship. It is not sneaky. It is wisdom to understand human nature, and never try to lead people further than they are prepared to go.

Keep it serious and dignified. Many times preachers get nervous during an invitation and think they need to get people's attention or try to get them on their side. (I'll never forget the time I heard a preacher do a Porky Pig impression during an invitation in a youth service. His attempt at, well, whatever it was he was attempting, was offensive to adults and ridiculous to teenagers.) Fear of embarrassment is one of the reasons people are hesitant to go to the altar. They need to have confidence that the preacher is not going to do something goofy or make a spectacle of them when they come forward. People are being called on to die to sin. This is, doctrinally, an invitation to a funeral, and those are solemn occasions. After the decisions are made for Christ, then it is time for celebration. But that, too, should be dignified. People should

never have cause to be embarrassed by something that happens in their worship service.

Think of the invitation as a series of gradually building and receding "waves." Knowledge of the process an invitation follows will give you confidence and keep you from getting nervous or embarrassed. Also, the congregation will know what to expect and this will be help, not a hindrance, to the pastor seeking to revive a dead or dying church. People are taught by repetition and consistency. A pastor owes those things to the congregation. Here is a "wave" approach that has been very successful in my experience. It is non-threatening, incremental, and helps people work up the nerve to walk the aisle:

At the conclusion of the sermon, ask the congregation to stand for prayer. The musicians should begin playing softly during the prayer. This means that they must be near the stage and be ready with their music. A musician who disturbs the invitation must be trained out of that tendency, and those who cannot be trained must be replaced (or you may just want to skip having live invitational music in favor of soundtracks or simple silence).

In the prayer, review the point of the message, asking God to help people respond to that issue after the prayer. After you conclude your prayer, immediately direct the congregation to keep their heads bowed and their eyes closed (the altar workers are exceptions to this directive). Ask the soloist to sing the invitational, and (usually) let him/her sing two stanzas. Signal the soloist to stop after two stanzas. The musicians should know to keep playing unless you tell them to stop playing. Ask the congregation to examine themselves spiritually for a moment. Ask for those who have a spiritual need to raise their hands and let you know of their need.

Again, the congregation will need to be directed to keep their heads bowed and eyes closed, and those raising their hands should be assured that only the pastor will see them. The altar workers aren't looking around. They are keeping their eyes on the altar worker director(s). The altar workers are keeping their eyes on the pastor.

Pray another short prayer, asking Christ to give courage to those who have raised their hands so they might come forward. Direct the music director to sing two more verses of the song, and ask those who raised their hands to come forward during those verses. It is rare for an invitation to go past four stanzas unless there is a major response. If someone has come to the altar that has been a spiritual concern to someone for a long time, it is appropriate to celebrate that. If there has been a large response, it is appropriate to sing a praise chorus.

Never hand over the altar service to someone else. Handing the invitation over to someone else disrupts the flow of the service that you have worked so hard to build. To put it another way, it breaks the rhythm. No one can deliver the invitation like the person who just preached the message. There is an artistic element to preaching that cannot be ignored. Preaching is a solo act, not a duet. You can't sing all but the last verse of a song, then hand it over to another soloist, and expect the audience to adjust. It just doesn't happen.

Dismiss the service in prayer. Call on someone to pray while you go to the back door. No one can shake hands at the exit like the pastor. This is a chance for you to make appointments during the coming week with those who demonstrated a spiritual need during the service or invitation. It's also a time of personal benediction and fellowship for the pastor. Never give that up.

Nothing is more important than the pastoral blessing.

A Matter of Preparation

Ushers must control the service traffic. As mentioned above, people are trained by television to sit still for about eight minutes, tops, and some people can't sit still that long. Until the pastor has trained the congregation, traffic in and out of the building will be a problem, especially if the church is reaching out to the unchurched. Visit any elementary school program, and you will see that many people have no sense of decorum. They have to be trained. So, a few simple recommendations are in order:

Babies and small children do not belong in the sanctuary, and anyone who thinks they do is either unchurched, ignorant, or does not have salvation and restoration as their priorities. A church without a clean, bright, well-staffed and well-furnished nursery and children's program is severely restricted in its effectiveness. As a matter of fact, it may never be effective at all if children are not cared for apart from the sanctuary. Nervous mothers are a bane to evangelism unless they are planned for. It may be a good idea for a section in the vestibule to be roped off for mothers who absolutely will not leave their children in the nursery. (Of course, the toughest chore then will be keeping teenagers and deacons out of this reserved area.)

The ushers should deal with disruptive people, or else the pastor will be required to deal with it from the pulpit, and that embarrasses everyone.

No one should be allowed to enter the sanctuary during a prayer or special song.

No one should be allowed to re-enter the sanctuary during last few moments of the sermon or during the invitation. The ushers will actually have to listen to the sermons on a weekly basis to be able to pick up on the pastor's rhythm, so they will know when he is circling for a landing.

Altar Workers. This has already been discussed above. The altar area must be kept ready for seekers. The altar worker director must be a person of wisdom and discretion. The altar workers must be trained and their training must be refreshed at least annually to prevent them from getting slack.

Follow-up Workers. If we are going to keep the harvest God gives us, we have to be ready to disciple those who come to the altar. The conversion to follow-up process must be seamless if people are not going to fall through the cracks. The pastor should promise follow-up (and explain what it is) when he asks people to come to the altar, and the church must deliver on it.

I am by nature a very shy person. I am not flamboyant, and don't really think well on my feet. I hate confrontation, and would rather do almost anything than press people to make a decision or tell people they are doing something wrong. Obviously, when I go into the pulpit, I go with a great sense of responsibility and accountability. And, invitations would be very difficult for me if I didn't stick to these basic principles on almost every occasion. The most important thing I have ever learned in preaching is the need to train the church to respect and value the altar, to get the altars open, and to do anything necessary to keep them open. God is not glorified by empty pews or by unused altars. His command to His servants is to see that His house is filled (Luke 14:23).

Even in California, a place everyone else in the United States thinks is filled with fruits, nuts and flakes, where I have lived and ministered now for 17 years, I notice that the churches that are growing through conversion, rather than through transfer, make a point of expecting people to make a decision when the claims of Christ are preached. It is encouraging to me to see that this is especially true in churches that target "Generation X."

I believe altar calls are ethical. I believe altar calls are effective. I believe altar calls are necessary to conversion growth. I believe God honors altar calls. I believe we are making a mistake if we leave them out of our evangelistic plans.

PART FOUR

Continuity

Turning a congregation around matters only if the change is long-term. The final section provides some direction for designing congregational advancement self-perpetuate.

CONTINUITY: UNDERSTANDING CYCLES OF GROWTH

To everything there is a season, and a time to every purpose under heaven.
A time to be born, and a time to die, a time to plant and a time to pluck up that which is planted.
--Ecclesiastes 3:1-2

Something I learned many years ago, early in my ministry, is that the church goes through various phases of a growth cycle just as a farmer works through seasons of the years in the growth cycle of the land and crops.

I was preaching a revival in a small country church in Northeast Missouri during the winter of 1969. I was staying in the home of a farmer, member of the church, and father of a missionary serving in West Africa. It was extremely cold, a good time to schedule a revival meeting in rural area of Northeast Missouri, just a few miles south of the Iowa border.

The farmer was engrossed in sharpening, repairing, remodeling, overhauling, and generally, just fixing his tools, tractors, wagons, and other instruments, vehicles, and farm implements. I found him out in a work shed, and asked what he was doing. He told me he was using the winter days, when it was to cold to work outside to get all these tools ready to be used when the weather finally changed. So I began questioning him about the work schedule of a farmer.

He told me there were four important seasons for the farmer in Missouri. Well, I already knew there were four seasons: spring, summer, fall and winter, but he put a new slant on the whole concept. Winter was for preparing tools, breaking up the ground and getting it ready for spring planting, and getting seed, fertilizer, and other necessary items ready for spring and summer. It was also the time for vacations. They spent time in the south land's resting and preparing themselves for the heavy work schedule that would come along with the other three seasons of the year.

Spring was the time for preparing the ground, planting the seed, and fertilizing the soil. This was a very busy time. It required help from all the family, and sometimes neighbors were called in to help. The rest of the year depended on the spring planting.

Summer was the time for watching, weeding, praying for rain and waiting. The seed germinated, grew, and progressed toward harvest. Soon fall came - the harvest time. Now the whole family joined hands in one gigantic effort to bring in the harvest. The livelihood of the whole family depended on it. New furniture, food, clothes, house remodeling, tools, and seed depended on the harvest success.

After hearing that, it appeared to me that the same cycles and seasons existed in the arena of church growth. As I have

Jim McAlister
REVIVING A DYING CHURCH

already said, I don't consider myself to be an organized thinker. In fact, I am usually quite a bit behind others in figuring things out, so this won't be earth-shattering news to most people. But it was to me, and it gave me a foundation on which to build in the future.

The seasons of this growth cycle are determined in many situations and areas by the weather. It becomes a natural procession from one period to the next because of the temperature. In other places it may be determined by the work schedule of the big majority of workers. For example, in rural areas where almost everyone is a farmer, the cycle will probably coincide with what is going on in the work force. However, in the area of Northeast Missouri, in 1969, winter was to the church a time for revival. Everyone was home, and it was too cold, and there was too much snow to do other things. In other places I have pastored, winter was the time to preach on needed church congregational problems, not revival. In Fresno, California winter is a part of the church harvest scene because the winters are so mild, and yet, work, school, and other things prevent people from traveling. They are available for church. Summer is the time for fixing tools, vacations, and fixing up your house.

In areas where a large corporation employs practically all the work force, that company determines the cycle, because they determine the work schedule. So it is easy to see that there are a variety of things influencing the cycle of a church. Every pastor and his church staff must discover the cycle and the things influencing it, but bear in mind, it's there whether you find it or not. No doubt about that.

So let's look at the cycle and see how it can be used. In fact, I've used it. Bear in mind that when I refer to winter or summer in the church cycle, I am not necessarily talking about the weather or the seasons; I am talking about one of the four periods of time in the church we pastor.

First comes winter. During the winter there are various reasons that you can't depend on all, or even a large segment of the congregation, being available to work at church or attend regularly. It may be due to weather, work, vacation, or even sports activities native to your area; but the crowd is not going to be in "growth mode." So during this time I preach on the great doctrines of the church. I teach about church organization. I talk about growth. And I set up programs for growth. I have training sessions. I deal with problems in the church. Recently I dealt with two important matters: a system to deal with the restoration of the fallen Christian, and a new system of deacon selection. We also established a prison ministry and organization and training for this ministry.

Church "winter" comes during the summer months in our area. During this time we plan on large groups of our people being out for vacations. We give our choir a two-month vacation. Our praise team members take vacations. Large segments of our congregation attend our denominational National Convention, so on at least two Sundays we get by with a skeleton staff. We conduct our family camp. Our college and singles groups have retreats. Our teens work in special needs camps. We fix broken buildings, rooms, facilities, and tools (computers, music instruments, and etc.), as

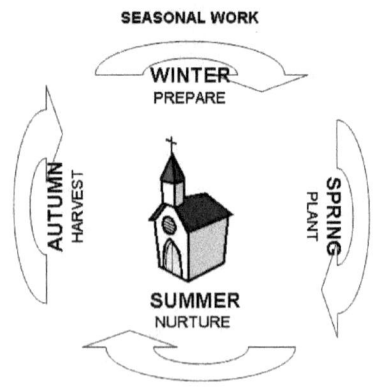

well as broken programs, organization and methods. We use this time to get ready for the next three seasons. We "break up the fallow ground," getting ready for seed planting.

Next comes spring. In our church that is October through December. During this time we start implementing the program and ministries we started during the season just finished. Our new prison ministry is getting started. We have had our training programs and now our staff is activating what they have learned and what they have instituted. We just hired a new evangelism and outreach pastor. He is getting ready to institute the program he brings to our church. The choir is back training and practicing. The praise team is all back on the stage. We have a revival meeting planned. Now this is a revival meeting not an evangelism event. We are praying and planning for revival. The evangelist for revival is a different type of preacher than the evangelistic preacher we have during harvest. In November the Friends Day committee is appointed, and under the direction of the outreach pastor. The pastor and staff start developing the Friend Day rally and attendance drive for spring. Big events during this season include the revival meeting, 9/11 memorial services, Thanksgiving services, and Christmas adult program, children's program, and full church Christmas celebration.

Next comes summer (that's winter in January through March in our church). This is the time of nurturing and tweaking previous plans. We are, during these months, promoting our Friend Days occurring in April. We will have an evangelistic meeting with a high-profile minister who will evangelize as well as promote the Friend Days and motivate our people to reach our goal that is usually tripling our average attendance. From this day's attendance and all the visitors (last year 400) we will have enough to contact for the next several

months.

Last is harvest. In our church it is April through June. During this time everything is geared to evangelism, soul winning, large attendance and church promotion. We try our best to not allow anything to interfere with harvest. No new programs are started. No big changes are made. We don't start any new buildings or remodeling. We evangelize, disciple, baptize and rejoice in what God is doing. Church decorating, outdoor advertising and all other facility improvements are geared for growth. This is harvest time.

We know that the four cycles of four seasons do exist and operate in our church. We don't let them irritate us or create problems. We have learned to use them to our advantage.

Once I discovered this fact of church growth, or lack of it, I started teaching and using it in every church I have pastored. The people must know what the pastor knows in this matter. Having learned this, we use it to the advantage of the church. This allows the church to always be caught up in every phase of church ministry. You can't have year-round harvest, and now that I know this, I don't get discouraged when growth is not really supposed to happen. There must be a time for sowing. You must have a time to deal with breakage: broken tools, disgruntled workers, plans that have crumbled, and other unhappy circumstances and personnel. Doctrine, priorities, missions, training, vacation, redecorating, all must be addressed, and a time allotted for each. When it is harvest time, it is harvest time. Put aside everything else and bring in the sheaves while you can (Romans 13:11-14).

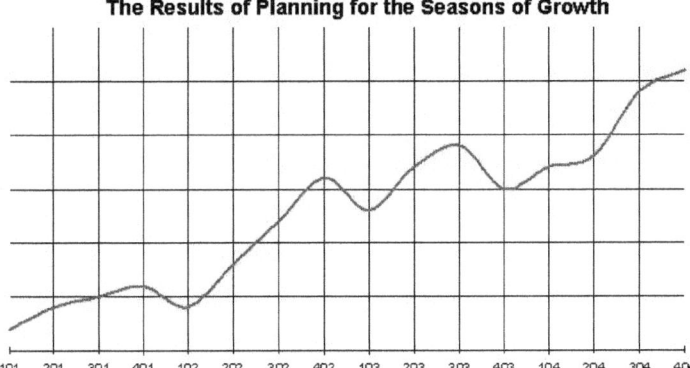

Taking the long-range view of the seasons of your church, and keeping good records, will enable you to anticipate the low participation months and use them to your advantage, capitalize on the high participation months, and produce overall progress.

CONTINUITY: MAKING THE CHURCH A CENTER OF INFLUENCE

And of the children of Issachar, which were men that had understanding of the times, to know what Israel ought to do; the heads of them were two hundred and all their brethren were at their commandment.
--1 Chronicles 12:32

Some people dislike the idea of authority. They only understand authority in terms of force or intimidation. Christians cannot operate that way. Fortunately, scripture provides a model of authority based on legitimacy and integrity (Romans 13:1-7). The authority a Christian church possesses is based on morality. This moral authority is influential.

Novelist Tom Clancy illustrated the ability to project authority with an explanation of the influence of an aircraft carrier to military tactics. According to Clancy, a 1000-kilometer circle (bubble) exists around an aircraft carrier, and nothing happens in that circle without the permission of the carrier air group (Tom Clancy, Debt of Honor, reprint (New York: G.P. Putnam's Sons/ Berkley, 1994, 1995), 497).

In a neighborhood, an influential individual can produce a "bubble" capable of projecting authority. Nothing can happen in that neighborhood without his or her permission or endorsement, sort of a "positive mafia." There may be a dominant business in an area upon which the economics of the neighborhood depend. Everyone watches out for that business and its facilities because everyone has a vested interest in it. Moral authority projects a bubble of influence that provides an inherent and powerful community ethic. I believe a church is missing God's call if it is not projecting a bubble of moral authority in the neighborhood in which it is located.

In the mid-1990s, the neighborhood around our congregation's property was in decline. The California Department of Transportation had purchased a lot of property just north of our church for the purpose of putting in a freeway. The houses sat empty for several years, and eventually became crack houses and havens for the homeless. As a result of this, our church's neighborhood was destabilized, with the usual increases in violent crime, burglary, and drug trafficking. Several cars were vandalized and burglarized in our parking lot during services, and the older membership began making noise about wanting to relocate to a safer area. At one point, the only entities still operating within a half-mile of our building was a liquor store to the west (liquor stores and small, run-down churches are usually the most stable institutions in declining neighborhoods), and a Seven-Eleven and plant nursery to our east.

All the other churches in our area had moved out. A police officer in our congregation told Fresno's mayor that we were considering relocation. He called me and asked if he could address our congregation. One Sunday evening, he spoke to us, and explained that we were the only stabilizing force in the area, because of our bus ministry outreach. If we left, there was no hope for that neighborhood. Our church voted to stay where we were, and our church began growing.

Some amazing things have happened in the nearly 10 years since the mayor visited us. During that time, we increased our bus outreach, began a gang ministry, two non-English-speaking congregations, a community food chest, a day care, an after-school program, and hired a full-time counseling pastor. All of our outreach concentrated on the neighborhood immediately surrounding our church. Our church has grown, through various ministries, to an average weekly attendance of 750 different people.

Some members left because we didn't move, but most stayed. (Our contention is that our congregation has never lost a member it didn't need to lose.) The freeway is being completed, and all the old empty shopping centers are being remodeled. Housing developments have gone in to our west, south and southeast, and another huge development is planned to our east. The old neighborhoods have turned around. Property values have increased dramatically. Including my wife and me, 8 church families have now purchased homes immediately south and west of our property. And, with the exception of a little mainline church full of senior citizens, a small charismatic congregation, and an old Catholic church, we are the only congregation in nearly a 5-mile radius. We are also the only congregation with any outreach.

I am aware that the most difficult hurdle for any church is hopelessness. We often feel overwhelmed by the sin around us, by the decline in the neighborhood around our church's property. Our small numbers compound our hopelessness. We don't believe a small church can do anything. We think there's no way to turn around.

It is important to remember that the Bible was written to point to salvation by using a very unique intellectual exercise. It was designed to provide the surrounding culture with an alternative worldview, one that would lead to questions about guilt, sin, morality, hope and salvation. Not only the questions, but also the answers, are provided by our Biblical worldview.

Isaiah understood the Lord's charge as one in which the message is to the masses, but not necessarily for the masses. God warned Isaiah that no one would listen to him, and would probably try to kill him. But the general public wasn't Isaiah's intended audience. He was targeting a minority, only those who could be influenced. The remnant was, apparently, "the only element in Judean society that was particularly worth bothering about…Isaiah seems finally to have got it through his head that this was the case, that nothing was to be expected from the masses, but that if anything substantial were ever to be done in Judea, the Remnant would have to do it." □

This "bubble" of authority around your congregation not only can be created by a minority, but also will only be created by a minority. They are the people with a sense of calling. This activity requires a sense of sacrifice, because, like Isaiah, Christians are often called to do things with only the Holy Spirit as a companion. Those trying to revive a dying church will walk through an extremely narrow tunnel with a low ceiling. On one side, they will be accused of not really carrying about people's feelings because they stress salvation over social gospel. On another side, they will be accused of intolerance because they "impose" their beliefs on the rest of the public when they refuse to give up moral standards in favor of sympathizing with those they seek to reach. On a third side, they will often be accused of not caring about the existing church because they stress outreach over member maintenance.

There really are people who use standards to justify selfishness. There really are people who attempt to impose a narrow interpretation of Christian holiness on everyone around them and alienate rather than attract those who could otherwise be reached. There really are people who have thrown out the demands of the gospel in order to do social ministry, unencumbered by doctrine and ministries they find tedious, distasteful, or intellectually embarrassing.

In nature, bubbles are created by "air." The inner pressure necessary to create a bubble of moral influence in a neighborhood around our churches is the Holy Spirit. Salvation is identified throughout scripture as the Holy Spirit's primary work (Genesis 3, Ezekiel 37, Acts 2). People who love God will not outgrow the salvation message. Without the salvation message, the church is just another group of nice people doing nice things. The identity of the church radiates from the mission of its savior, seeking and saving that which was lost. Without the mission, the bubble deflates.

A bubble is a projection that provides the qualities of community, authority, integrity and discernment to a neighborhood. It is the result of the church as a "moral center" in a neighborhood. It is a moral climate, a community ethic, a culture of revivalism.

The church is the moral center of the projection. It has the ability to create a community, authority, integrity and discernment. It can only project moral authority if it is actively reaching the lost in its neighborhood. It is extremely doubtful that a citywide bubble can be produced. Cities are just too big for the relationships to jell sufficiently. Bubbles of influence have to be created by individual churches with interpersonal relationships built around Christ. Neither can a bubble be created by drive-in memberships. It is only feasible if the people doing the ministry live in the area around the church.

The ministries of the church are the effects of the church's moral authority bubble. They strike at specific targets or problems in the neighborhood. They include spiritual gift-based ministries, including speaking ministries (preaching, teaching, evangelism, etc.), service ministries (food and clothing distribution, tutoring, medical care, day care, all designed to influence people with the salvation message through day-to-day contact); structure ministries (participation in neighborhood clean-ups, neighborhood watch, etc., which teach good habits and demonstrate Christian values as a means of creating a hunger for the message), stability ministries (marriage, financial, substance abuse counseling, teaching Christian values), and sign ministries (neighborhood pastoral care, recreation ministries, ceremonialism). These ministries are goal-directed. If a church is to exert moral influence in its community through evangelism and discipleship, nothing can be tolerated in the church's ministries that do not fulfill the mission of the church. The church is where they land, refuel, and get repairs.

Once the bubble of influence is created, how may it be maintained? What keeps it inflated? What protects it from sharp objects? More important that "helping" is a church's responsibility as a "moral" force- a distinctly Christian moral force. Attention must be paid to current events and public mood in the neighborhood, but parties and mood swings should not be allowed to alter the fundamentals of the church's mission, which are found in the word of God.

A church must maintain its moral influence in its neighborhood, because a church without moral influence isn't really a church. Once it obtains that necessary moral influence, it must learn to exert it in a moral way. Nehemiah is a good example of an ethical exercise of moral influence. He did so through effectual prayer and a genuine relationship of trust with the King of Persia. A mayor doesn't have to be a Christian for Christians to pray for and support him/her spiritually. If a mayor's policies and/or actions are unjust, prayerful influence should be exerted by Christians to lead him/her to reconsider those policies and actions. The mayor should not be threatened with a loss of political support. The mayor should be made conscious of the prayers on his/her behalf, and, through the integrity of the Christians who are praying for him/her, be led to value that support. Artaxerxes not only cared for Nehemiah; he also valued Nehemiah's influence with his God. Spiritual influence is "good" lobbying, and it needs two qualities.

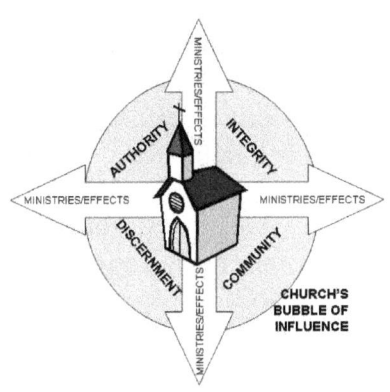

Each church must see its neighborhood as the community to which its people have been called by God. When a church is a patron to its neighborhood it shows preference for it, watches out for its interests, and takes its problems personally. A calling to a community means taking responsibility for it, protecting it, and promoting it.

At the same time, it is important to remember that churches have a unique sense of difference. God's people are

always strange people in a strange land. It is not unreasonable to consider the world as occupied territory, and the church as the sojourner. The church is not to "go native." It cannot overly identify with the culture in which it resides.

It is vital that a neighborhood church have a personal stake in its neighborhood. It is far too easy for a congregation to feel good about their ministry to their neighborhood because they maintain property there, even though they don't see the building between Sundays. That is where their "church" is. They hire ministers to have an office there, who are always home before dark. When the neighborhood gets too bad, they can always relocate the church to the suburbs, which is where the supporting membership all lives, anyway. People want a church convenient to their homes, so their kids can go to church with their friends. If anyone is won in the old church neighborhood, they worship with people they do not know when they get there, and that won't last long. A basic rule of group dynamics is that, if there are two fundamentally different sub-groups within one large group, eventually one will eliminate the other.

A church that abandons its neighborhood for a more controlled suburban setting presumes that the neighborhood is beyond hope. The difference between a church that exists for itself and one that exists for the lost is a sense of calling. To fulfill the calling involves the economic and moral

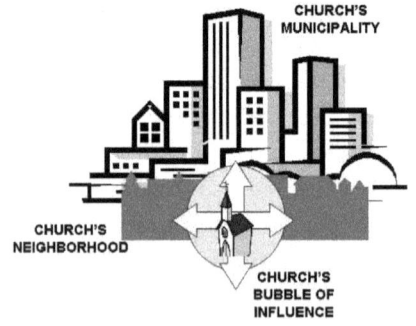

preservation of neighborhoods through evangelism and discipleship. Evangelism requires proximity, because people don't like crossing socio-economic barriers to come to Christ. Sticking to one's own kind is a naturally sinful thing to do. Christians contradict the sinfulness of segregation by accepting their calling to be people, not peoples.

To win and preserve neighborhoods, they must first become "our" neighborhoods. Nehemiah refused to utilize his budgetary allocations and underwrote some expenses of reconstruction himself, because he desired to create a personal stake for himself in the rebuilding of Jerusalem. It wasn't a project he was going to abandon easily. This act also created a reputation for integrity in the eyes of the government and the people of Judah. Because of this, Nehemiah had the credibility to publicly confront those who were extorting from the poor. His personal investment prevented Israel from becoming dependent on federal outlays. When Nehemiah called for a 24-hour watch, he could do so unapologetically, because he was the first person up every morning, the last person to bed every night, and did more than his share in security and construction responsibilities. When Ezra declared days of mourning and celebration, they were effective; not because they were holidays, but because they were "our" holidays, like they were "our" walls, "our" temple, and "our" law.

Establishing a moral climate will not be accomplished by substituting therapy for soul-care. The recognition of the importance of the religious in psychology is welcome, but it is more important that psychologists know Christ. Without Christ, religion is simply a necessary neurosis, a psychological placebo. Christ brings the power of the Holy Spirit to literally heal souls.

That the church is a moral force in society should not be in question. The belief that morality is the key to peace and well-being has been question for several decades. One neighborhood at a time, churches should reestablish the superiority of Christian morality, and should not hesitate to stress its superiority.

In the New Testament, a word frequently used to specify the effect of the Holy Spirit is power. The Greek word is *dunamis*, from which the word dynamite comes. When an explosion takes place, the actual force or power of the blast is from air. The air around the blast point is pushed away instantaneously, faster than it is supposed to move. It compresses upon itself as it travels away from the center of the explosion, moving, shaking, or destroying everything in its path. However, after all the air is blown away, especially when fire is involved, it also creates a vacuum. The air immediately is sucked back into place.

The church that obviously cares about its community will be needed by its community. Neighborhood needs can revive a congregation to some extent, because the church will realize that it is relevant. This power will move, shake and destroy some things around the church. The power that leaves the church naturally creates a vacuum, and the atmosphere that went out will come back. A church that is operating in the power of the Holy Spirit goes out in power, and then comes back in the same power. It scatters and gathers. The blessed community around it is jolted by the blast, and then is gathered in to the point closest to the power.

This kind of dependence on the Holy Spirit will make churches centers of influence. These points not only bring new life to a congregation, but to the neighborhoods and communities that surround them. Eventually it will have an effect on the whole surrounding region. Read the stories of Joseph, Jesus and Paul and the books of Ezra, Nehemiah and Esther for great examples of building influence in adverse circumstances.

The use of power is always painful to someone. Congregations are often concerned about the expenditure of resources without return. When the Holy Spirit's power goes out in a blast, the vacuum it creates brings in resources. Pain is not a good enough reason not to go forth in the power that God has given us. If it were, Christ would never have gone to the cross, and Paul would never have evangelized Europe and Asia Minor. And no pastor would ever have planted a church to begin with.

CONTINUITY:
TESTING THE LEADERSHIP

If the foundations be destroyed, what can the righteous do?
The LORD is in his holy temple, the LORD's throne is in heaven: his eyes behold, his eyelids try, the children of men.
The LORD trieth the righteous; but the wicked and him that loveth violence his soul hateth.

--Psalm 11:3-5

I taught pastoral students at California Christian College too long to say that I actually enjoy testing students. I really don't. In spite of my reputation, I'm a very soft-hearted person, and I don't like to make people feel bad. Nevertheless, I always had to test them, because that's where you see what they've learned. I believe God tests us like a teacher tests a student.

This scriptural list of tests faced by pastors and other leaders isn't meant to be exhaustive, but since the Bible bothers to mention them, we can assume they are normative. These people all failed their tests.

RATIONALIZATION: Abraham was the patriarch of the people of God, the Friend of God. God had made a great three-fold promise to him: land, a blessed existence, and many descendents (Genesis 12:1-3). God had not delivered yet, except for the fact that everywhere Abraham went, those with whom he came into contact were blessed by God and Melchizedek, king of Salem had blessed Abraham. His wife was nearly 90 years old, and there was still no heir. It's hard to be the father of many nations if you aren't a father at all, so Abraham's wife made a proposition to Abraham- that he have a son by her maid. That was a common practice in the Middle East in those days, so he agreed, and Hagar had a son, Ishmael. And then Sarai, Abraham's wife, actually got pregnant, and demanded that that boy would not be heir with her son. The complications from that decision continue to this day and plague the whole world.

The principle of leadership testing here is maybe the biggest one of all: God does not run on our schedule. He has His own timetable, and His own chosen vessel. We are inclined to take shortcuts to expedite matters, or circumvent integrity to get our way. God always keeps His promises. However, the maturing of the servant is a more immediate concern to Him than hurrying with His promise- that He always keeps.

RESENTMENT: Aaron and Miriam, Moses' brother and sister, were leaders in the traveling Israeli refugee nation. Like many pastoral families, the members of the family tend to serve in leadership roles in the congregation their relative pastors. Also, like many relatives of pastors, they let family issues bleed over into leadership issues. They did not like the woman Moses had married because she was Ethiopian. This, of course, we would identify as bigotry. Because of that dislike, they cast aspersions on Moses' judgment and leadership (Numbers 12:1-16). "Hey, God has spoken through us, too. What makes Moses so great?" God struck Miriam with leprosy, and Aaron, the priest charged with going to God for the people of Israel, went to Moses and begged him to have the curse listed. So much for challenging Moses' special place with God. It was fairly easy to challenge Moses- until he needed someone with a special relationship with the Lord.

The principle here is making a distinction between disagreement and challenge. No one is so wise that disagreeing with him or her from time to time isn't proper. God does work through all of us- Aaron and Miriam were right about that point. But that is a far cry from challenging the pastor's leadership over a personal bias.

FRUSTRATION: By contrast, the next story demonstrates that Moses was not faultless. He was God's deliverer, God's appointed man, the one with the power. But frustration is a common hazard in all leadership, and maybe especially in the pastorate. Moses' complaint to God is really human- I can hear myself saying it: "These aren't my kids! They're yours! Why to I have to listen to their whining?" (Numbers 11:10-15) Later, when they ran short of water, they organized against Moses and Aaron, and accused them for talking them into going out into the desert to die (Numbers 20:1-13). God told Moses to take his rod, and speak to the rock, and water would come out of it. By this time, Moses had had it. Instead of talking to the rock, he challenged the people: "Listen, you rebels! Do we have to bring water out of this rock for you?" Then he struck the rock with the rod twice. And even though he didn't follow God's instructions, even though he

basically acted like it was he and Aaron who were producing the water for Israel instead of giving credit to God, water still came out of the rock. But God spoke to Moses and Aaron and said that because they had shown a lack of faith in Him and did not "hallow" Him in the eyes of Israel, they weren't going to get to finish the trip. Their leadership would be incomplete because someone else would lead Israel into the Promised Land.

How many times have we played the "It's God's will" card to get what we want? God's authority is not an ace up our sleeve to pull out whenever we want to show who's boss. We cannot justify misbehavior or sanctify personal preference by abusing our position as pastor.

FEAR: Joshua was Moses' successor, appointed to lead Israel into the Promised Land. The problem here was a lack of closure. He didn't complete the occupation, even though that was God's clearly specified will. At the end of his tenure, he receives this assessment from God: "Thou art old and stricken in years, and there remaineth yet very much land to be possessed" (Joshua 13:1). He was sent to occupy, but just didn't carry it out. The Israelites were content to get a foothold, and Joshua didn't lead them any further.

The fact that people don't want to do much is why leaders are necessary. People who want to be led are no real trick to lead. You basically have to watch them to make sure they don't get in over their heads. Getting people to do what they otherwise would not do is the essence of leadership. Leaders don't depend on the constituency and consensus they find. They gather a constituency; they build a consensus. It's hard to say someone failed if they never really tried. This was obviously God's concern about Joshua from day one. Four times in his anointing to lead he was admonished to be strong and courageous (Joshua 1:6, 7, 9, 18). He wasn't strong. He wasn't courageous. He didn't lead.

NEGLECT: Eli was a priest who had a typical pastoral problem: offspring who used their father's position for their own benefit and shamed the entire ministry (1 Samuel 1:12-17, 22-25; 4:17-18). Eli was judged by God because he didn't discipline his children, and his judgment consisted of God disciplining Eli's sons Himself. It is not uncommon to find pastor's wives and children who absolutely hate the ministry or simply refuse to be supportive of their husband or father in their efforts. There have been lots of articles written advocating different degrees of obligation and involvement in a local congregation for pastor's families. Sometimes a pastor fears losing his children or alienating his spouse so much that he may put off making the disciplinary decisions necessary to have a happy home. The fact is that children learn to work by helping their parents. All kids who grow up on farms learn to work by helping their parents. I've known electricians, mechanics and plumbers who take their kids along with them on Saturdays or during summer days and have the kids hand them tools, sort out screws, load paint in the truck, etc. Why is it such an invasion of the pastor's family's time for the pastor to take them along with him as he visits, administers, or prepares for services?

I always tried to take one of my kids with me whenever I visited someone who had children. My child would play with the children while I visited with the parents. Granted, it usually cost me an ice cream cone on the way home (and sometimes that's the only reason they went), but my children learned the value of ministry. And I find that whenever I take someone

with me now as I visit, I always end up treating them to a soft drink or ice cream or coffee. (One of the perks of being a Christian is that food is part of our doctrine!- Acts 2:46) I also didn't specify what my wife would do in church. If she wanted to be a leader of the women's group, that was fine. But if she just wanted to attend the group and get fed, that was fine, too. My wife actually decided that she wanted to start a children's church when our children were small. Now most of my grandchildren are out of high school and my wife is still leading one of our children's churches. She's in her 35th year of children's ministry right now. I'd hate to try to pull her out of there. (Most of the kids who ride our busses think Helen is the pastor of Harmony Church.) Children need exposure to ministry and holiness and integrity. No one is going to teach it to the pastor's kids except the pastor.

TERRITORIALISM: Saul was God's nation-builder, the first king of Israel. God had given Israel a king because they insisted. He warned them in terms of taxes and war, but they still persisted. The first king he chose was taller than anyone else and generally regarded as a wise, humble man. But, as so often happens with successful leaders, they become authorities on everything in their own minds. They build a good Christian education program, and soon they're telling painters how to decorate, travel agents where they ought to go on vacation, and college professors how to teach. Saul didn't just want to be the political leader of Israel- he wanted to be a spiritual leader, too. And he wanted to be the spiritual leader. Samuel the priest had instructed Saul that nothing was to be spared when the Philistines were defeated, but Samuel was late getting to the post-war meeting and Saul decided to take a hand. He offered sacrifices from the condemned sheep and spared some of the leaders for public derision. When Samuel arrived he discovered what Saul had done and informed him that God's judgment would be the loss of the kingdom from his family. There would be no Saul dynasty (1 Samuel 13:1-14). Posturing steals the glory from God. I don't think that God refuses to share His glory because He's selfish or egomaniacal. I think he refuses to let us share his glory for the same reason you don't give loaded guns to monkeys.

CONFLICT OF INTEREST: David is another man who refused to discipline his children. He made the mistake that many pastors make, as we've mentioned above. He put his family above the welfare of the nation. He wanted to keep his son's love. He wanted to keep it so much, he indulged Absalom so much, that Absalom decided that David was a doddering old fool, not to be taken seriously, and needed to be replaced. He launched a rebellion against his father and had him run out of Jerusalem (2 Samuel 18:1-18, 33-19:8). Even when Absalom was proven a traitor, David gave strict orders that he was not to be harmed (which his chief of staff disobeyed). If a man is so concerned about his family that he puts them before his duty, his option is stepping down and letting someone he can trust take the reins. It doesn't look like David ever considered letting anyone else be king. He just hoped against hope that Absalom would straighten up and like him again. It is a great tragedy when men and women leave God's service because of the behavior of their children, but it is an equal tragedy when they stay in ministry and allow their children to destroy their ministry with their behavior. It is also wrong when a pastor allows the ministry to usurp the rightful place the pastor owes to his children.

COMPROMISE: Solomon, the man who replaced David, was Israel's Philosopher-King. Solomon was practical. He wanted to preserve the economic success of his reign, and chose the route everyone else chose for guaranteeing peace. He made marriage covenants with other kings by marrying their daughters (1 Kings 3:1; 11:1-13) and probably giving his own daughters to them or their sons, although I haven't noticed that in Scripture. After a while, these women "turned away his heart after other gods; and his heart was not perfect with the Lord his God…- 11:4). Compromise isn't always bad- it is often the method God uses for testing motives and filtering out selfishness. Solomon's mistake was compromising the wrong things for good reasons. He outgrew the principles that had qualified him as king of Israel in the first place- wisdom and whole-hearted devotion to God. He became devoted to other gods through his wives' influence, and started confusing being wise with being shrewd. And we know how all these things came out- check Ecclesiastes. Old ministers often do not want to take risks. They want to be known as "elder statesmen" and have the dignity and honor that comes with age and wisdom. Also, they aren't quite as quick as they used to be and can't think on their feet as well when someone disagrees with them. So they begin compromising on the spiritual leadership that made them honorable in the first place. Don't get me wrong- plenty of younger pastors and leaders do this, but somehow it looks worse on someone whose whole life has been devoted to serving God until they get worried about losing what they've got. Self-preservation is not bad; it's just not God.

AUTHORITARIANISM: Rehoboam is, unfortunately, typical of someone who gets placed in a position of authority for the first time and let it go straight to his head (1 Kings 12:1-16). The nation of Israel split almost immediately and some of the tribes were lost to history. He is a good example of a novice (1 Timothy 3:6). Respect has to be earned, and congregations have to be constantly reassured that you pastor them because you love them. I suppose some pastors just fall in love at first sight when they are exposed to a church and never get over it. It always took me awhile to be in love with a church- we had to date for a while. And then one day, when I talked about my home church, I realized I was thinking about the church I was pastoring at that moment instead of the one I had left.

In like manner, it takes a while for a church to accept you as pastor after they have elected you. I have found, in my own experience and in conversations with other pastors, that the 6th year is usually the watershed. That's the year when some people who have been withholding their support give in and start following you- they trust you not to leave them. And others who have been withholding support realize they aren't going to be able to wait you out, and they leave. Usually there are a number of families attending that you have led to Christ yourself. At that point, the church will have a kind of natural feeling of excitement that can be utilized to build momentum for growth. The pastor who comes in with both barrels blazing is going to run out of ammo really quick, and stands a really good chance of changing nothing but his address.

SELF-PROMOTION. Judas was the treasurer of the first apostolic band (fill in your own joke here). He took advantage of his position for personal gain. That didn't last long, and it never does. Sooner or later you wonder what you're really getting out of a situation, and decide to take steps for either revenge or increased gain. When you read the gospel accounts

in a harmony of the gospels, a number of things become apparent. The breaking point for Judas appears to have been the anointing of Jesus by Mary. When she anointed Jesus with the expensive perfume, Judas complained that the perfume could have been sold and the money given to the poor (John 12:1-8). John confides that Judas didn't really care about the poor, and reveals that he simply resented not having an opportunity to steal the hypothetical proceeds of the sale. Jesus rebukes him. In Matthew's account (26:6-16), several of the disciples are mentioned (not by named) as thinking this was wasteful and Jesus delivers a rebuke. But Matthew mentions that Judas sought out the chief priests and offered to sell Jesus to them. When Luke tells the story of Judas, he doesn't mention the anointing or Mary, but says that "Satan entered into" him and he went his way and "communed with the chief priests and captains, how he might betray him unto them" (Luke 22:1-6).

So here's the summary: Judas was embezzling from the disciples. When he saw an opportunity to get access to perfume worth a year's salary get poured over Jesus' head, he complained by "spiritualizing" the act as wasteful and harmful to the poor. Jesus rebuked him. He was humiliated and angry because he had been called down in front of the other disciples and because he probably realized that Jesus knew what his real motives were. He wanted to get even, and at that point Satan entered him, and gave him the idea of offering to sell Jesus to the high priest. When people are serving Jesus for what they can get out of it, sooner or later they are found out as a mercenary and react with bitterness.

OTHER INTERESTS: Demas is famous as the associate pastor who quit for selfish reasons (Colossians 3:14; 2 Timothy

4:10). We generally haul this out when someone doesn't like his salary, but that's unfair. Jesus, who warned against depending on money when doing ministry (Luke 10:4) also specified that pastors should receive sufficient remuneration (10:7). Usually assistant pastors quit because things just aren't the way they thought they were going to be. They don't have the relationship with the pastor they crave or maybe they don't have all the authority they think they need. Demas left for a "love of the world." That meant there was materialism involved. He had other interests. What's worse is a pastor who has other interests that consume him (politics, sports, his computer) and doesn't leave the ministry. He basically uses the pastorate as a way to do as he pleases, receive a salary, and have no accountability.

COMPETITION: Diotrephes is an example of a church boss. Church bosses are usually people who have learned not to trust pastors for very good reasons. They are often advocates of the "Fool me once, shame on you; fool me twice, shame on me" school of thought. They may have actually had to save a congregation themselves several times, and, since they love their church, they aren't willing to leave it in the hands of someone they don't know. Previous pastors have fallen short or refused to actually pastor, so they said to themselves, "Okay, I'll be the pastor." Maybe they like the church just the size it is and oppose growth because they figure they're going to have to take care of it again when the latest pastor leaves and if the church grows it might not be manageable. On the other hand, they may simply be people like Diotrephes- they love to have the preeminence. Maybe they are used to running things wherever they are and can't stop it when they get to church. Or maybe they get pushed around everywhere they go and

decide that at church, at least, people were going to listen to them. So they challenge the pastor's authority any time they get the opportunity. There's nothing less Christian than a power struggle.

These are common occurrences in churches. We've all heard of churches going through them. We can expect them.

Our leadership will be tested sooner or later. --You've been warned.

CONTINUITY:
KEEPING THE CHURCH BALANCED FOR THE FUTURE

...Ye, being rooted and grounded in love, may be able to comprehend with all saints what is the breadth, and length and depth, and height; and to know the love of Christ, which passeth knowledge, that ye might be filled with all the fullness of God.

Now, unto him that is able to do exceeding abundantly above all that we ask or think, according to the power that worketh in us, unto him be glory in the church by Christ Jesus throughout all ages, world without end. Amen.

--Ephesians 3:18-21

The basic life of an institution follows this sequence: (1) Man, (2) Movement, (3) Machine, and (4) Monument. This is true of schools, businesses, government agencies, clubs and even churches. This just happens naturally. No one really plans it. But we can plan for it.

Man

In the beginning, a church is all about leadership. When a church first starts, it is, often the dream of one person, or one small core group of people. That was true of Harmony Church. A few people followed a leader to start the church. Everything goes along fine at first. Everyone is excited. Decisions are easy to make. You don't have to wait for a committee meeting or a vote. Everyone is very clear about who the leader is, and everyone is personally loyal to him. It is usually the pastor, but it could be a very kind, dynamic, gifted lay person who is the central figure of the group.

Another thing about a church like this is that it is small. Everybody knows everyone else, where they live, what they do for a living, and who all their children and parents are. That's one of the things people like about the church. You already know everyone's likes and dislikes. And, being small, it's easy to control. On the other hand, the loss of one significant person can devastate the group- maybe even kill it.

If a group gets larger than 60 people, one person can't really control it with relationships anymore. That's why a lot of churches remain "Mom and Pop" enterprises, with the pastor handling all the ceremonial things and his wife handling the politics. Other people who would have liked to run the church will realize that there's only room for one leader, and they will drift away. If they don't leave, they may become jealous and unhappy, and if that happens, they will probably stay that way. Other people adjust by buying into the leader's vision. As the vision is realized, more people come, and there is a greater need for more leaders, and then dissatisfied people become satisfied because they feel needed.

Movement

Sooner or later, if the pastor is an interesting preacher and the people are friendly and not clique-oriented, the church is going to actually grow past 60 people. The momentum of a group that isn't encumbered by rules, regulations, policies and budgets is attractive to a lot of people. Some people just hate organization. But they love the excitement of a new endeavor. They like the way there are new people at church every time they come, and they invite their friends to come, because "this isn't like other churches." And, they like the idea that the church is actually on the move, that there seems to be a point to the services. It hasn't hit a rut yet.

On the other hand, some people who were attracted to the church primarily because of its smallness and intimacy will drift away in search of intimacy somewhere else. Some of these people who are attracted by intimacy, though, will become integral leaders or participants in small groups in the church, like the choir, a visitation team, or a Bible study, and this will satisfy their intimacy needs.

Machine

Eventually the congregation has to begin making big decisions. The group has outgrown the house or garage or backyard in which it has been meeting. The church has to decide whether they are going to become a bunch of different cell churches, meeting in one large group only once or twice each year, or whether they are going to rent a larger facility, like a school cafeteria, storefront, or another congregation's building for an afternoon, evening, or weeknight service. This means that the church has to get a checking account to pay the rent, and, in order to have a checking account, the church has to have a board of trustees to sign for the account. The group

may decide to build a new building, which requires all kinds of organization.

The church will have to obtain a 501(c)(3) number so people can tithe and it will be tax deductible. The church may decide to elect a full-time pastor at this point, or hire a secretary, and that means paying taxes, which means getting a tax number. People may decide that a formal membership structure is necessary.

Eventually, it will become very difficult to handle all the needs of the children who attend. Curriculum will have to b chosen, for Sunday school and children's church, which will require a review committee, or maybe a Christian Education Board. Tables and chairs will need to be purchased, unless the congregation is renting a school facility. No matter what, the church will require organization each week to set up the rooms for worship and education. Since people expect professionalism from their churches these days, a sound system will have to be purchased, and, since those are very expensive pieces of equipment, the church won't want to let just anybody run the system, and so technicians will have to be appointed. That will require a vote.

Members will notice that a lot of people visit one or two times and then disappear through the cracks. Someone will suggest that a visitor's committee should be started to keep track of them, send them letters, and maybe go visit them.

The congregation or the pastor will reach the conclusion that they need policies and procedures, boards and committees, and a lot of people who came to the church because of its easy-going, casual approach to church will drift away in search of another church with fewer obligations. However, some people will be attracted because of the fact that the church is organized and looks like it handles problems

(Acts 6:1-7). While there are a lot of people who hate organization, and even think it is unspiritual, there are also a lot of people who think it is sinful to be disorganized.

Memorial

Once a church gets policies and procedures, it has established a means of self-perpetuation. Members are dependable, carry on the mechanics of the church business, raise budgets, hire pastors, care for facilities, etc. The church is maintained, and nobody really stops to ask what the purpose is anymore. It is assumed that everyone just knows.

After a church has been in existence for 20 years or so, it is inevitable that a member will die, either through natural causes, or maybe through some tragedy. Or maybe the founding pastor retires, or someone makes a large endowment to the church. It is common for someone to suggest that a building be named for the deceased person, retiring pastor or generous benefactor.

Nobody really notices, but at that point, the church has made a decision that will limit growth from then on. There is no longer any flexibility in this congregation. Instead of innovation and imagination they have policies and procedures. Instead of vision for the lost, they have financial responsibilities. Instead of a desire to accommodate needs of people, it has a sentimental attachment to a building that will control decisions from that point on.

Dangers

Each stage is necessary, and each stage is natural. Each step also has inherent dangers, if a component at that stage is allowed to dominate instead of merely being a stage.

Man-stage dangers. One person can control a group to

the point that no one else has any say. If a church grows a little, this can still be a problem- one group can do all the controlling, and cancel everyone else's influence out. The primary danger of this stage is dictatorship. This kind of situation can limit the church's ability to grow, its desire to organize, and its ability to become stable.

Movement-stage dangers. A desire for excitement or intimacy can limit a group's vision. The lost cease to be a priority. It may become a dictum of the church that disagreement is a sin, and so important issues are never discussed (a good way to hide sin in the ranks). The danger here is co-dependence. There may be an unhealthy, dysfunctional cliquishness that allows group members to exclude others because of a deformed sense of "intimacy."

Machine-stage dangers. A church can become bound and gagged by committees, policies and procedures. The danger here is fear. The budget may become to focus of the church, rather than a tool to accomplish the church's goals. It may be very difficult to integrate new leadership, because the old membership is tried and true, and no one wants to take a risk. Innovation looks pretty good in other churches, but not here. That's the NIMBY argument against doing anything messy.

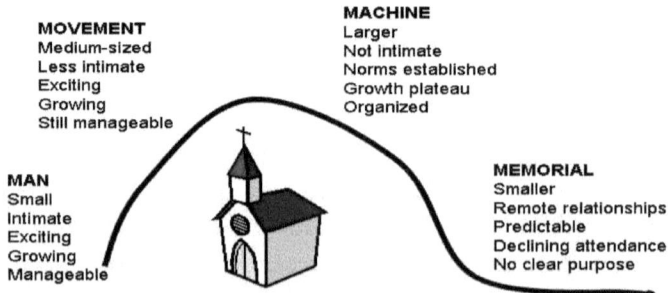

Monument-stage dangers. Finally, a church may reach a place where the best days are all behind it, and all the members have left are their memories. The danger here is survivalism. Tradition is much more important than growth, discipleship, or vision. Everyone knows that something is wrong, but no one wants to bring it up. Depression is rampant. This church is actually a vampire, sucking the life out of everything and everyone around it, or like the ghosts in the movie: "They don't know they're dead... they only see what they want to see."

Strengths

These steps are normative. They are considered to be valuable, necessary and logical. Every church, organization, club and company will eventually recognize its needs for leaders, strong relationships, policies and procedures and traditions.

Man-stage strengths. A church has to be developing leaders constantly. If a church intentionally develops leaders, this practice prevents one person from being able to take over. It also provides a large pool of leadership in case one significant person leaves. The strength of this component is discipleship. There is only one indispensable person in any church, and that person is Christ. Every leader must be weighed in terms of his or her devotion to the Lordship of Christ as well as leadership ability.

Movement-stage strengths. A church has to do things that encourage people, meet people's spiritual needs, give people vision, and provide opportunities for growth and ministry. The security of this component is fellowship. The church has to do things that emphasize and expand the church's relationships.

Machine-stage strengths. A church needs to constantly

review the policies and procedures it has to make ensure their viability and still contribute to its mission and purpose. The security found in this component is wisdom. It's very easy for an institution to become a victim of its own desire to be efficient. All our methods for growth have to be measured, not only be our purpose, but also by wisdom.

Monument-stage strengths. A church must establish traditions. While the man and movement give a church its focus, and the machine gives a church its structure, the traditions of a church provide its identity. The security of this component is principle. This is where doctrine is identified. This is also where the church calendar is determined. These are all traditions that tell others and remind us of exactly who we are.

Using the Process to Keep the Church Refreshed

These things happen in an institution because they are all needed. Each step builds on the previous step. The goal is to prevent a church from dead-ending as a memorial, and to avoid the dangers at each step of the way. The way to avoid hitting a dead end is to turn the process into a cycle instead of inevitability. What is the church doing each year to strengthen these areas, to maintain a cycle of growth?

Using the Man stage. In order to build upon the strengths of leadership instead of becoming hidebound with "good ol' boyism," a congregation has to consistently developing new leaders. This means risk-taking. Training must be provided, opportunities for service must be offered, new ministries must be welcomed within the church and spiritual entrepreneurship must be encouraged. The more leaders a church has, the more it can do. Leaders are much more important than finances.

Using the Movement stage. The Psalmist says that the

Lord places the solitude in families. For some people the most important thing about the church is not the answers it offers, but the inclusion it provides. Venues for church fellowship must be provided, and that takes a lot of imagination and hard work. Small group needs must be taken care of. Everyone in the church needs a group in which they are known and valued. Church unity doesn't just happen. It must be intentional. It must be planned for.

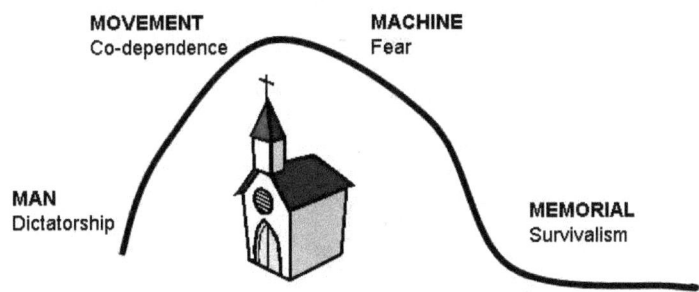

Using the Machine stage. Policies and procedures must make sense. Less trouble does not mean more sense. If it's a really good policy, it will probably take a lot of work to develop. The budget has to be a tool. No one can afford to let their budget make their decisions for them. Getting control of a budget means more than controlling spending. It means making the budget work for the church instead of against it. It especially means making sure the budget doesn't become the "permission-giver" for ministry development. Boards and committees need checks and balances. In our current arrangement, the standing rotating boards (Deacons, Trustees, Christian Education) are required to submit requests to a council that is completely replaced each year: the Stewardship

Council. That means that the Church budget has both the benefit of experience (from the standing boards) and a fresh perspective (from the Stewardship Council).

PROVIDING BALANCE AT EACH STAGE

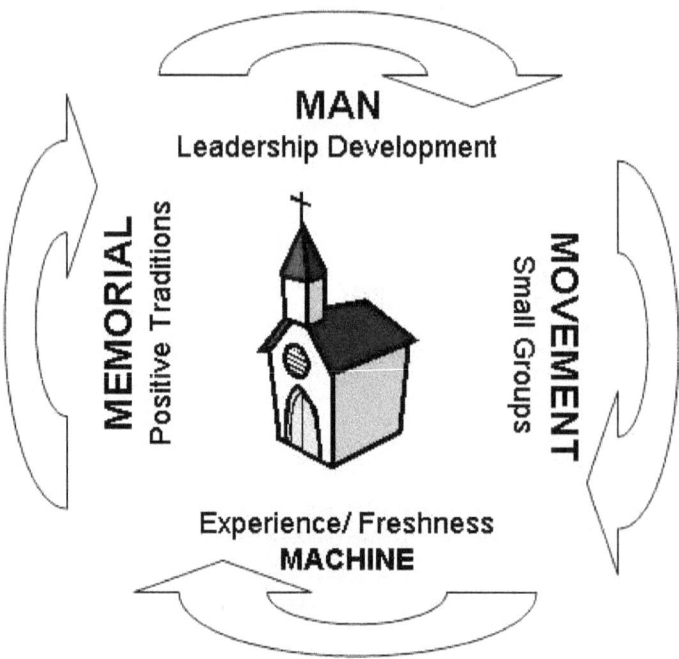

Using the Memorial stage. Traditions must be established that promote the church's vision and purpose. Sentimentality cannot be allowed to be the determining factor for church tradition. Traditions cannot be allowed to prevent a congregation from making necessary changes or decisions for enhancing the church's commitment to God's will.

Jim McAlister | 183
REVIVING A DYING CHURCH

One of the incredible things about the gospel of Jesus Christ, which is really unique among the world's religions, is how acceptance God's truth does not rest upon a suspension of observable experience (the resurrection of the dead not withstanding). As I mentioned in a previous chapter, churches can be observed to follow basic seasons of planting and harvesting. Perhaps that's why Christ chose those metaphors when He explained the Kingdom of Heaven in Matthew's gospel.

The study of organizations such as businesses and governments can give us quantifiable patterns that we can either surrender to or utilize for further growth. We know these things happen because we can commonly observe them- they are normative. Because of that normative quality, we can depend upon them and plan for them, not be taken captive by them.

Tradition is not the enemy unless it is the end- that was the real "church" philosophy dispute Jesus had with the Pharisees. Jesus said nothing of the word of God would pass away, and the beneficial traditions remained in the church as well. (See Dr. Robert Picirilli's discussion of the worship services in the Diaspora synagogue system in *Paul the Apostle*. How much of that is present in

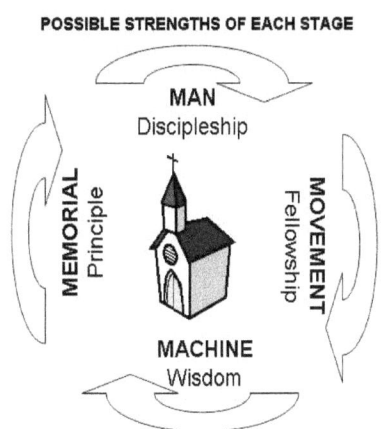

Christian worship?)

We can count on tradition to accomplish the positive things that only tradition can accomplish, and to take over if we let it. We can count on the man, movement, and machine stages to do their jobs and to support one another. We can count on the regular opportunities God gives to till, plant, nurture, harvest and store the fruit. God has provided all these lessons for many reasons.

CONTINUITY: OBEYING THE WHOLE COMMISSION OF CHRIST

All power is given unto me in heaven and in earth.
Go ye, therefore, and teach all nations, baptizing them in the name of the Father, and of the Son, and of the Holy Ghost;
Teaching them to observe all things whatsoever I have commanded you; And lo, I am with you always, even unto the end of the world.
--Matthew 28:18-20

I want to conclude this work with some comments about the local church's responsibility for evangelizing the whole world. Any church that is really alive will eventually develop a hunger for broadening its impact. As I've approached my "golden" years, one of the most exciting developments has been the way Christ has enabled me to participate in missionary work in South Korea, Russia and the Ukraine, and has allowed me to work with Korean, Ukrainian, Russian and Chinese students and immigrants to the United States. I have never been more excited (or more confused, when I'm the only person in the room who doesn't understand the language being spoken).

The need to extend our church's influence throughout the world through evangelism was formulated by Christ Himself in Acts 1:8. In simples terms, that command offers a typology for cross-cultural evangelism. (In this model, "E" stands for "evangelism.")

E-0 Jerusalem: evangelizing people in our immediate area (friends, family, etc.).

E-1 Judea: evangelizing people in our culture, who are not in our immediate area.

E-2 Samaria: evangelizing people who operate in our culture, but are substantially different from us (different language, different background, different socio-economic status, etc.).

E-3 Uttermost: Evangelizing people of a different culture and in a different nation. (Adapted from Donald McGavran, *Understanding Church Growth,* revised, Grand Rapids: Eerdmans, 1970, 1980, 70-71.)

This model would correspond to the following applications:

E-0   Relationship-based evangelism.
E-1   Church-based evangelism.
E-2   Cross-cultural evangelism.
E-3   International evangelism.

It is obvious that the church makes the families of existing members a priority in its evangelism (although membership continues to drop), and makes foreign missions a priority. Those related to church members receive some attention, but those in different cultural groups within the community are more or less ignored evangelistically. The neighborhood church lost steam after the 1950's, as commuter churches became the norm. Those churches that moved to the suburbs (and further and further from the inner-city, as time went on)

tended to survive. Those churches that did not move tended to decline because the ethnic makeup and safety of the neighborhood changed, and the remaining congregations tended to gray out.

Evangelism receives equivalent allocations in church budgets. We spend most of our money on us- membership maintenance, plant maintenance, and salaries. Very little is spent on the neighborhood or community, unless those allocations can include existing members. World mission gets the dregs, if that. Fortunately, due to the changing nature of neighborhoods, churches that survive are, more or less, being forced to engage in cross-cultural ministries. What was cross-cultural a few years ago will be mainstream in the very near future. Caucasians are rapidly becoming simply another piece in the "marvelous mosaic" that is North American culture. One day there will be no national majority, only regional majorities.

It is my contention that a church will not be able to sustain vitality if it does not reach out into all of these spheres, because to do otherwise is disobedience to Christ's great commission. We do not have a holistic, Christ-honoring evangelistic vision unless we are reaching into each of the four areas effectively. In like manner, pastors will stop growing spiritually unless they are reaching outside the responsibilities for which they receive compensation to do something they don't have to do, but want to, just because they want to present a gift of service to God.

A neighborhood and community-based emphasis presents a problem. Cross-cultural evangelism requires specialized training and is often politically difficult to manage-especially with a graying church constituency who has little in common with their current neighborhood demographic in

terms of age, ethnicity and economics. A dying church will only be legitimately revived if the neighborhood around the church is understood and reached.

I believe that applying our churches' spiritual gifts to evangelism will increase our understanding of the potential lying dormant in our churches. This potential, if tapped, will enable us to do everything else I've suggested in this book. If scripture is to be trusted, we can say assuredly that each congregation has a gift mix sufficient to bring glory to God, build a church, and reach the lost (Romans 12, 1 Corinthians 12, Ephesians 4, 1 Peter 4). We're going to use a new term in this chapter: congregation capacity-building, which I suppose was coined by Bruce Bugby (*What You Do Best in the Body of Christ*, Grand Rapids: Zondervan/Willow Creek, 1995, 61). The old term for this is volunteer ministry. We want to use

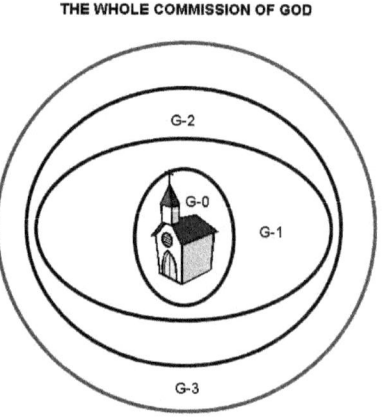

this different term to emphasize that evangelism is done best when it is church-based, but not church-centered. We want our churches to be the sending unit, not only in foreign missions, but also in neighborhood outreach.

In this scheme, we'll change the "E" to "G" (gift utilization) and make the following applications:

G-0   Church-centered utilization of spiritual gifts for evangelism. All the spiritual gifts are prioritized at this base level. This is what usually happens if a congregation utilizes spiritual gifts at all. It is not to be disparaged, since a firm theological understanding of spiritual gifts and vigorous organization and utilization of those gifts within the church is the first and most essential step in increasing the capacity of any congregation. In the long run, the proper understanding of spiritual gifts and their place in the church will probably produce more stained glass windows and other expressions of art and beauty, since believers will receive encouragement to express their passions within the body of Christ. Bringing glory and honor to Christ will correlate with the growth of the body numerically and financially.

   G-1   Neighborhood-centered evangelism. The most essential spiritual gifts at this level are: administration, apostleship (i.e., mission's leadership), craftsmanship, discernment, encouragement, evangelism, faith, giving, helps, hospitality, leadership, mercy, pastoring, preaching, and wisdom. Utilizing these gifts for evangelism makes a local congregation an essential and influential part of the neighborhood in which it is located. The church exercises the moral authority mentioned in the previous chapter in the neighborhood. In order to do this, the church must demonstrate a vital concern for the neighborhood surrounding the church, best done by simply being the "presence" in the area.

Neighborhood churches, through maintaining a caring and evangelistic presence in their own neighborhoods, break the usual mold of neighborhood churches, which usually remain oblivious to their surroundings. They can proactively exercise the legitimate, prophetic authority to create a new norm- especially in declining neighborhoods. They can create a "spiritual infrastructure" through congregational capacity building, which can diminish crime by evangelizing criminals through their children. They must genuinely serve the neighborhood so that the residents of the neighborhood, whether they attend the church or not, consider it to be their own church. The moral authority envisioned here could be considered a "public ethic," or possibly esprit de corps. Whatever it is called, its function is the projection of a moral climate into the surrounding community. Basically, it implies that the neighborhood is better off with the church than without it. People know they can get physical help there, and this opens the door to evangelism. It makes people more willing to listen to the gospel message.

G-2   Community-visioning sharing of spiritual gifts. The most important gifts at this stage are: administration, craftsmanship, creative communication, discernment, evangelism, giving, helps, intercession, mercy, and pastoring. This is an intentional involvement in the spiritual welfare of the entire community (town, city, metroplex), in which the church resides, reaching people of different socio-economic-ethnic backgrounds, sometimes (not always) a significant distance from the whole church's ability to be involved. Most churches do not have enough people to make a significant impact in their community in terms of specialized ministry, but since every church has all the gifts, there are bound to be people in each congregation gifted for cross-cultural evangelism.

However, these believers may become very frustrated if they don't find roles in which to utilize their gifts, and may lose confidence in their congregation as "irrelevant," or may move on to another church in which they see an opportunity to serve. Outreach is very intimidating to many pastors. They may feel that they barely have enough workers to manage the program they have at present. How can they afford to send members outside the church, where their loyalties may be divided and their interest in the local church may wane?

Acts 13 provides us an example for the church as a sending body. When God moved upon the church at Antioch to send out ministers, they commissioned the two best teachers they had, not the people they could afford to lose. Barnabas and Saul were their candidates. Church-based commissioning for community visioning is manageable and will bring glory to God. This could solidify the connection between ministering members and the congregation, and would emphasize the ministering member as the representative of the congregation to other cultures.

When designing your cross-cultural outreach, you should first identify which spiritual gifts are not being utilized in your congregation in a way that satisfies members' senses of calling and passion. This will define and enhance your congregational capacity.

Next, you should investigate various missional (parachurch) agencies in the community, because there are some things you are not going to be able to do in your own capacity, and you are going to need advice, or you may need to build a coalition in the neighborhood. Decide who you can work with. (There are different levels of cooperation, which have been articulated well by Dr. James Westgate, founder of the Fresno Leadership Foundation, church planter, and mission's professor at Mennonite Brethren Biblical Seminary.)

Many people have no interest in building coalitions because of a past emphasis on ecumenical unity - this is where very diverse groups and traditions try to come together. I get frustrated with these because one has to become morally neutral to really find unity that everyone can agree to.

Emphasizing mission means that we agree on a special

project to work on together, but we all maintain our own particular beliefs, which is pluralism in its best sense. I have participated in many of these and have found them to be profitable. However, it is difficult to cooperate with other groups in evangelistic efforts, because we may not agree on the process or message of salvation. It is much better if we join with other declared evangelicals when trying to do an evangelistic outreach. If we try to join together to create a drug rehab program there could be fewer problems. In light of these two issues, there are three levels of working together:

1. Coordination, which requires the minimal of relationships and simply means we are bringing efforts to the table for a common goal. It requires minimal accommodation or compromise.
2. Cooperation, which requires that we each bring something to the table and expect something from the table in order to get our goal accomplished. It requires a moderate amount of accommodation and compromise.
3. Collaboration requires us to not only bring something to the table but also have a common bond or relationship to get the goal accomplished. It requires a heavy amount of accommodation and compromise.

Christians must be careful to decide (1) which of these are they going to work on and (2) can a sub-group work on a different level without destroying the whole group. For example, we could coordinate with Catholics in a march against abortion as long as they were not requiring us to compromise our stance on the gospel. We could collaborate with others who have the same theology and philosophy that guarantees that we do not compromise our commonly held gospel in a drug program. But there are some levels of cooperation that cost too much. They require us to give up principles that define our view of Christianity. If we do find a group we can work with, we can initiate collaboration with them to fill a particular niche for our gifted members. We can commission members to serve with that agency, and support the agency with prayer and finances.

And, we should continually teach the holistic concept of spiritual gifts utilization; i.e., that believers and congregations must maintain a ministry activity at each level of evangelism to be balanced, growing entities.

G-0 The Ends of the Earth. This is where "foreign missions" comes in, and this is where many churches have a greater money-to-member ratio than in any other ministry. The church that emphasizes utilization of spiritual gifts in areas of passion consistent with the ministering member's personality style will develop more candidates for ministry. Mission agencies are parachurch in the classic sense of the word- they do that which churches cannot or will not do. With the advent of mega- and meta-churches, more congregations can commission and send out missionaries supported solely by their own budgets, but usually a mission agency of some type is necessary to deal with governmental issues. Missional agencies are not seen as a threatening entity in the foreign mission context, because pastors know that relatively few of their members are going to identify a passion for international ministry. Emphasizing the spiritual gifts, personal passion and personality style triad, however, may change the frequency of missional call.

Observing all of the Great Commission will change the way individual congregations view themselves, their neighborhoods, communities and the globe.

A FINAL WORD

Throughout this book I've tried to make a case for reviving the dying church using practical suggestions undergirded with spiritual truth. I hope I've accomplished that, but just in case I haven't, let me briefly state what I meant in each of the chapters, and include a scripture or two that I hope will inspire you to ponder the direction God may have for your church.

It is important that we understand two things: that many churches are dying, and that many of them can be revived. Although Ichabod is written over the door of many assemblies (1 Samuel 4:21), many of the problems with many churches are not spiritual. They are, instead, problems of a lack of wisdom, a lack of organization, or a lack of vision.

In light of that, it is important to consider the role of the pastor in reviving the dying church. The truth of the matter is that no church will be revived without active, wise, bold leadership. Without pastoral leadership, there is no direction (Ezekiel 34:1-6).

However, as important as the pastor is, you're not much of a shepherd if you don't have any sheep. The lay leader's role in reviving the church cannot be overestimated. Discipleship in the pulpit is no more essential than discipleship in the pew. Nothing much gets done without the laity. Without the laity, the leader has no one to transfer his vision to (Nehemiah 4:6).

Incrementalism is the key to reviving a church. Single, significant, spiritual steps must be taken to begin a slant toward

revival. The pastor's first responsibility is to inspire hope that there is a future possible, and he must do so by doing what he alone can do- lead spiritually (1 Chronicles 12:32).

Along with the spiritual changes come the concrete decisions. Practical steps must be taken to program the church for revival. There are important decisions to be made, and philosophical and cosmetic changes to be undertaken before the church can be revived (Matthew 3:1-3).

No church can change with only one leader. All or most of the congregation's leadership must be prepared to undertake the vision and communicate it to the rest of the church. The pastor should never be the only person who understands the vision. The whole leadership of the church should understand it, agree with it, and teach it to everyone else (Mark 3:13-14).

The Church is an intentional institution; that is, God had a specific purpose in mind when He ordained it, and He has a specific purpose in mind for the church you are attempting to revive. He has provided safety for it (Matthew 16:18), a privileged position for it (Ephesians 5:23), and a particular mission for it (Matthew 28:18-20). As we build it up, we have to stick closely to His plan (Ephesians 4:11-13).

A church can be organized into efficiency, but it can only be spiritualized into revival. It is important that a church's revival be founded upon the purpose for Christ's coming- to call all to repentance. That is why I believe it is necessary to concentrate on opening the altars of the Church as the central focus (2 Chronicles 7:14; 1 John 1:9).

Understanding the cycles of farming helped me understand the cycles of Church growth (Ecclesiastes 3:1-15). Once I understood these things, I was able to relax (there is no point in beating your head against the wall about the harvest when there's snow on the ground). It also helped to me to be prepared when the time was ripe for reaping souls.

If a church isn't known in its neighborhood as a place where help is available, it isn't a church that follows the image of our Lord. If a church doesn't make its neighborhood a better place to live in, it isn't doing much in the way of holiness. If a church doesn't influence its neighborhood or community for Christ, what is it doing? I believe that a revived church will be a center of influence in its community (Genesis 22:17-18).

A church must keep itself balanced for the future by constantly strengthening its leadership and purpose (Matthew 28:18-20; Acts 6:3; 13:1-4; Ephesians 4:11-12), its fellowship (Ephesians 4:14-32), its practices (Acts 15:1-35; 1 Timothy 2-5), and its traditions (Exodus 12; 1 Corinthians 11:23-34). These things must be constantly monitored, and no one thing can be allowed to dominate.

Every Christian, Church and pastor must obey the whole commission of Christ by doing things outside their normal parameter of service, extending to world missions, but also to spiritual warfare on behalf of their whole city. It is too easy to be a professional Christian, doing only what we are paid to do (Luke 17:10). We only grow when we stretch.

I wish I had known all these things many years ago. I wish I had twenty more years of active service to give to God. However, I'm now older and have to rely on younger people to listen to my words and glean what they can from them. I hope you can see past the mistakes in this work and get a good grasp on my experience in the service of Christ. I hope you can learn from it, improve upon it, and bring glory to the Name of Christ and glory in the Church. If that happens, I'll know that God has truly blessed my life's labors. May God richly bless you as you seek His guidance in reviving a dying church.

Jim McAlister
REVIVING A DYING CHURCH